Ahmed Fayek was an associate professor of Clinical Psychology in Cairo, Egypt, before immigrating to Canada.

His interest in psychoanalysis was a major factor in his immigration to Canada in 1971. He had an accredited training in the Montreal Institute of Psychoanalysis and became a training analyst in 1980.

He was Director of Psychology at the Royal Ottawa Hospital, before retiring in 1989.

In the last fifteen years before fully retiring, he did some consulting and supervising work in the Middle East and dedicated the rest of the time to writing and publishing.

To Jack, Sophie, and Alex.

Ahmed Fayek

PSYCHOANALYSIS: A THEORY OF THE HUMAN SUBJECT

AUSTIN MACAULEY PUBLISHERS™

LONDON · CAMBRIDGE · NEW YORK · SHARJAH

Copyright © Ahmed Fayek (2020)

Ordering Information:
Quantity sales: special discounts are available on quantity purchases by corporations, associations, and others. For details, contact the publisher at the address below.

Publisher's Cataloging-in-Publication data
Fayek, Ahmed
Psychoanalysis: A Theory of the Human Subject

ISBN 9781645751519 (Paperback)
ISBN 9781645751502 (Hardback)
ISBN 9781645751526 (ePub e-book)

Library of Congress Control Number: 2019917692

www.austinmacauley.com/us

First Published (2020)
Austin Macauley Publishers LLC
40 Wall Street, 28th Floor
New York, NY 10005
USA

mail-usa@austinmacauley.com
+1 (646) 5125767

Table of Contents

Preface

Early analysts and several weighty thinkers, with penchant toward psychoanalytic thinking, recognized and documented a great deal of facts about the nature of the human subject. Learning about the subject – as such – was triggered by psychoanalysis in the first place and it remained its core endeavor for several decades. However, it gradually seized to be the only source of that knowledge because of the psychoanalysts' insistence on limiting psychoanalysis to the profession of psychotherapy, meanwhile the theory of the subject was getting expanded and enriched by contributions of other human sciences. A worrying gap opened, and is getting wider, between psychoanalysis and the facts about the subject that other equally capable authorities are gathering.

A genuine interest in this issue would reveal a major problem that is rarely addressed. Although psychoanalysts claim to be the legitimate heritor of psychoanalysis, by virtue of being its only practitioners, they did not and still do not have a defined theory of their practice. There are few recommendations about practice in the theory, and the analyst has to rely on his experience in didactic personal analysis and rare remarks usually exchanged in the rest of the training activity. However, the rest of the theory of psychoanalysis has all the elements of a theory of practice, but only if analysts notice and accept that psychoanalysis is not a theory of psychopathology but a theory of the subject as an epistemological entity. In better terms, psychoanalysis is a theory of the subject that could succumb to psychoneurotic conditions in the course of his life. When that happens, and the subject seeks psychotherapy, the therapist has to know first what the healthy condition of the subject is. Physicians have to learn the anatomy and physiology of the healthy person before they advance to the stage of medical practice. Without a theory of the subject – as a healthy being and a subject matter in his own right – psychoanalysis is a useless base for any practice of psychotherapy.

Introduction
Point of View

The IPA, since its inception in 1910, went through many crises, which were – at the beginning – mostly caused by personal conflicts among its members. The personal conflicts evolved to be considered theoretical differences. The theoretical conflicts – as expected – took the form of crises. The crises were a mixture of personal conflicts, theoretical disagreements, and some serious attempts at controlling the IPA movement. In periods in the fifties, the sixties, and in North America in the seventies too, the classical theory of psychoanalysis was 'free for all' to criticize and suggest modifications. Things deteriorated because the differences were *not* considered legitimate results in a developing science and a changing profession.

The IPA was becoming aware of the gradual disintegration of the theory of psychoanalysis. The splits within the local societies, almost everywhere, and the notion of schools of psychoanalysis which emerged in the USA in the late sixties of the last century overwhelmed the IPA. In 1989, Wallerstein – the president of the IPA in that period – suggested accepting theoretical plurality as a politically expedient solution to the impending danger of the breakup of the psychoanalytic organization. His plea was not officially accepted but was pragmatically recognized. Thus, the IPA was saved by lowering its criteria of accrediting the previous local and regional societies and made it easy for the new ones to join. The splinter societies, with their training institutes, were and still are common additions to the IPA membership, without an open scrutiny of their credibility.

In 1995, the IPA acknowledged that psychoanalysis was going through a serious crisis of credibility and that it is time to revise it (Cesio, 1995). The crisis in 1995 was different than the previous ones. It was related to a steady decline in the number of patients who sought psychoanalytic treatment, and the number of young professionals who sought training in the profession of psychoanalysis. It was also of global nature and not pertaining to particular conflicts, like the crisis of the 'controversies' in Great Britain in the early forties of last century (King & Steiner, 1991), or local circumstances in one region like the crisis of Lacan in France. The members of the IPA's committee for the study of the crisis agreed that the state of the theory and training play an important role in the creation of the crisis, in addition to some external factors like social and economic changes that did not exist before in a manner that would affect psychoanalysis. However, they neither agreed on the nature of the theoretical factors and the flaws in training systems that have a role in the crisis, nor offered meaningful remedies to the situation. The leader of the committee, after reviewing the different reports prepared by different psychoanalysts from different regions of the IPA, concluded that: "A plague such as the one we psychoanalysts are facing today is a pandemia comparable to the one that descended on Thebes because of the murder of Laius, the father. And now: could it be [the crisis] the result of the murder of Freud, the father? Will we not discover, like Oedipus, that we ourselves are the murderers?" (Cesio, 1995, p. 2).

The presumed solution of accepting theoretical plurality to avoid the declining status and influence of psychoanalysis reveals a dormant problem in the discipline of psychoanalysis. Traditionally, the protection and survival of the IPA was considered the safeguard and the means to maintain psychoanalysis itself. Freud and the pioneers were anxious and keen to maintain and enlarge the IPA as the guarantee for the survival of psychoanalysis. We inherited from the pioneers the view that the IPA, i.e., the organization, is capable of sheltering psychoanalysis from both internal and external threats. This attitude was and still is clearly flawed. The existence of psychoanalysis was the 'raison d'être' of creating the IPA, and not the other way around. Furthermore, psychoanalysis is *living thought* that will naturally keep developing, changing, and recreating itself. Therefore, the organization(s) of psychoanalysis has to adapt to psychoanalytic change and progression, otherwise it will cause its demise. This is what was disregarded and avoided in discussing the ongoing crisis of psychoanalysis because (to my mind) analysts did not consider any solution that would replace the IPA to start with. They thought of saving the organization and not its subject matter.

What about psychoanalysis itself!

There are main issues to address when we pay attention to psychoanalysis: Could the crisis be a result of a deteriorated psychoanalysis, and parallel deterioration in its training? Could the IPA be ignoring or avoiding facing this possibility? Could the IPA has become an inadequate organization to be entrusted with the future of psychoanalysis? Is it possible to continue learning and training in psychoanalysis the way it was done a hundred years ago: Those issues require, and even demand, that psychoanalysts move their loyalty from the institute of psychoanalysis to psychoanalysis itself? Psychoanalysts have to pay attention to the nature of contemporary psychoanalysis and work on what is essential to make it as useful and inspiring as it once was.

To do that with an effective result is to look at two things involved in the contemporary crisis of psychoanalysis: The state of psychoanalysis *itself* and the process of qualifying the practitioners of psychoanalysis.

Chapter One
Functionalism and Structuralism in Psychoanalysis

Freud kept modifying his theory till the end, implying continued discontentment with his theoretical formulations. He left us with what was named the structural theory of 'ego psychology.' It was considered by most analysts as his last theory, especially that he merged aspects of the topographic theory in this new theory in an effort to bypass the absence of the unconscious in its formation. It took few years after his death and some hesitant attempts by few analysts to be critical of that metapsychology, erroneously called the structural theory. The dissatisfaction even got worse as it created several internal crises on the regional level. Although they did not contribute anything new to the crisis of 1995, they extended the sense of disappointment with the theoretical condition of psychoanalysis. Some analysts dealt with those internal theoretical crises by suggesting some adjustments to an already unacceptable theory. Some others tried to rephrase aspects of the classical theory as a measure of improving it. The notion of 'schools of psychoanalysis' was insidiously established.

Since those two approaches have failed, and still fail in changing the situation, we should leave the theoretical offshoots aside and concentrate on what psychoanalysis is meant to be in the first place. Better, we should find what all those theoretical formulations have in common, including Freud's metapsychologies, to identify the underlying flaws that are affecting contemporary psychoanalysis. It is not difficult to find what all those divergent theories and schools are about because we have a good lead to understanding this problem in Freud's consistency in approaching the issue of theory. Freud's endeavors from the day he diagnosed hysteria as suffering from reminisces (1895b) to the day he said in the *Outline:* "We have discovered technical methods of filling the gaps in the phenomena of our consciousness, and make use of those methods just as a physicist makes use of experiment" (1940a, 196–197), had the hope to turn psychoanalysis into a systematic method of explicating psychical phenomena. He wished to get to a theory based on causes *and effects* that could explain psychical phenomena in the same manner theories in physical sciences do with physical phenomena. His cathartic theory – as his more or less a first comprehensive notion of a theory – was explaining psychoneurosis as a function of the repression of reprehensible ideas and feeling of mainly sexual in nature. Whatever the change or improvement he introduced to any of his following theoretical formulation, it was always an ambitious attempt to find better functional causes to the more complex effects that he kept encountering in the expansion of psychoanalysis.

There are two points to highlight in that regard. Nomothetic sciences are founded on functional[1] discoveries, in which causes for physical effects are uncovered to *explain* the physical world. Human phenomena (idiographic sciences) defied all functional explications despite the diligent attempts to reach that objective since the beginning of thinking about the human subject. Freud, as part of the scientific culture of his time, sought after this illusive functional theory of psychoanalysis. Intuitively, he knew that the unconscious dynamics of the intrapsychic core of human phenomena would preclude a true functional theory of the psyche, because the unconscious as part of the link between the causes and the effects in any human affair has no consideration for the cause-effect links. Nevertheless, and because this was the rule in the scientific world at that time Freud persisted and kept trying; he had no alternative.

Contemporary psychoanalysts cannot anymore continue seeking functional theories of psychoanalysis. Since the early years of the last century, human sciences and psychoanalysis too, joined an upsurge of change in the theoretical approach to human phenomena. The upsurge is branded as 'structuralism.' Early in the century de Saussure, a linguist, was teaching in Geneva a course in linguistic, which was totally different from anything that was done before, and his disciples published his work in 1916. He revealed something that we – as homosapiens – live, experience and do without awareness in our daily life when we speak. To speak we needed a language, and our spoken languages have proven to be structures that dictate the manner we talk. The structures of a language are unconsciously acquired and assimilated thus makes speaking possible; not only in the verbal sense but in the communicative sense (a smile says something). However, he managed to reveal the core of the discovery, which was that language is made of signifieds (concepts) and signifiers (sound-image) and the link between them is purely

---

[1] Functional theories are about the link between causes and effects in phenomena studied where an effect is a function of a cause.

arbitrary. There is no physical requirement that dictates the choice of the signifier of any signified (the spoken language). Yet, the arbitrariness of the link between the signifier and the signified, which is different in the different languages, does not affect the structure of the *spoken*. The spoken is always either a metaphor or a metonymy of the signified. Expressing the signified in those two linguistic modes is also unconsciously determined.

Thinkers and philosophers extended structuralism to become the new and different approach in the humanities. Saussure uncovering the existence of a structure in such a universal phenomenon like speaking a language, encouraged thinkers in the humanities to try that principle in their fields too. Structuralism revealed that human phenomena could be understood not only when described as functional phenomena[2]. Since the late sixties and particularly in the seventies of last century this approach reached its zenith, when the humanities expanded the issue of structuralism to look at other human phenomena that are part of human communications (symbols and signs). Hence, human phenomena were no longer looked at as mere 'givens,' but manifestations of the workings that create them as formations. They were not seen in the context effects that have causes. The notion of an unconscious structure behind speaking made thinkers, philosophers, human scientist change their approach to the human phenomena.

Structuralism was born in the thirties and the forties of last century. So, psychoanalysts faced the appeal of joining the structural movement and letting go of functional thinking and metapsychology as theoretical framework. The shift to structuralism was easier in some parts of the world like the Latin countries but not the Anglo countries. However, there was no avoidance of structuralism because it is the fabric of our daily dealings with each other: we try to find the meaning of what we deal with and tend to consider what we understand as the cause of the matters at hand; we are continually looking for meaning to what we say and what is said to us by guessing the link between the signified and the signifier. Nevertheless, structuralism – in its specific and theoretical connotation – is not just that. It deals with something particular about homosapiens: *we are of dual existence in everything that we are*: we are manifests that have latent natures. We are the subject who is us but also the object of our existence, the active *I* and the observing *Me*. Our psychical life is what is there within our dualities or between the manifest of us and our latent nature.

---

[2] Temporarily I mention dreams as a psychical phenomenon that could be explained by the day residues and understood as a manifestation of the psychology of the wish (see chapter three).

We have to ask ourselves: if structuralism makes us understand our nature and if psychoanalysis is the science of understanding 'selves,' how could Freud have discovered psychoanalysis decades before de Saussure revealed structuralism?

Scholarly examination of the Freudian text shows something that was not missed by the scholars: every time Freud came to a theoretical formulation, he sensed that it is not what he meant to say. He was – unknowingly – never satisfied with functionality as theory of the psyche but managed – reluctantly – to make it fit in the concept of psychotherapy, which was and still is synonym with psychoanalysis. I mention now, and will explicate later, two features in Freud's theory which attests to his 'latent' structuralist approach to the theory. Freud was of the opinion that the 'normal' should always be the basis of a true theory of psychoanalysis. His revision of the concept of the unconscious and identifying the systemic unconscious (1912d) and the non-repressed unconscious (1923b) put the unconscious in a structural format (see chapter eight). His insistence on translating what symptom say as if they are psychoneurotic texts is the intuition of a "structuralistic" analyst. His clinical tripartite protocol of anonymity, neutrality, and abstinence shows the importance of staying with the structure of the patient's condition and not his motivation (see chapter ten). The vocabulary of structuralism was very important in distinguishing it as a distinct theoretical modality. Unfortunately, it was not available to Freud at his time. Therefore, the term psychoanalysis is usually associated in the minds of people with a profession of psychotherapy.

In the minds of psychoanalysts, this term means what they learn and train to practice in their training institutes. Psychoanalysis, in that context, does not seem to have an origin beyond Freud's efforts and genius of discovering it. Ordinary people are not aware of the degree psychoanalysis has penetrated their daily life and changed it. Psychoanalysts miss the impact the theory has brought to the original human sciences, and the insights it brought to the professions of psychiatry, clinical psychology, and social work. The mental health disciplines are no more able to function without the notions of psychodynamics. Nevertheless, there is little if any attention paid by psychoanalysts to the origins and expansions of psychoanalysis beyond its psychotherapeutic capacity. *Psychotherapy is the tail and psychoanalysis is the dog.*

It should have occurred to at least some of the psychoanalysts that psychoanalysis would not have had such unusual effects on the *Western Culture* in general if it did not have deeper roots in that culture than just Freud's endeavor. In a way, it could be said that psychoanalysts should have realized that Freud's discoveries needed to be revisited and rediscovered – many times over – because despite the changes introduced to them over the years, his works continue to give us different and better insights in human nature than anything else. The aspiration to make 'Freudian' psychoanalysis give more could be supported by a short account about its link with the Western culture in general through its philosophical heritage.

The birth of organized philosophy in the seventeenth century started a great interest in the 'human subject' and generated rich philosophical discussions about his nature and attributes. A chain of thinkers who attempted to understand the subject discovered that everything they explored about him was dual in essence. They realized that whatever they identify and define about the subject seem to be entwined with its opposite. It was getting clearer – since the age of philosophy – that the subject was not a simple ontological 'thing' like other things that fill the world; his was a special phenomenon of dualities and gaps between the duos of those dualities. However, the dualities of the subject came to an impasse when philosophy failed to discover what could bridge that gap within those dualities. Opening that impasse came from Freud himself when he initiated the psychoanalytic movement. The duality of consciousness and unconsciousness caught the attention of the intellectuals. Psychoanalysis seemed to be coming up with the lacking link in the chain of the philosophical efforts to identify and define the subject. However, that duality seemed to be limited – in psychoanalysis – to a technique of psychotherapy. This early bend in its route of evolving turned it into a new professional field of mental health, rather than a continuation in the field of discovering the human subject. This type of birth left an indelible mark on psychoanalysis. The mark concealed its true nature as a new expansion in a theory of the subject.

Psychoanalysis's approach to the issue of the subject and his dualities was surprising and unique. Freud, different from the thinkers who preceded him, came up with the distinctive knowledge of the subject as a being with an intrapsychic life (a structure), which distinguishes him from the rest of other beings. The phenomena of the intrapsychic came first from the field of psychopathology and elementary endeavors to improvise a method of psychotherapy. After endless efforts by Freud and the psychoanalytic organization to confine psychoanalysis to a theory of psychotherapy, psychoanalysis proved to be more than a mere profession that is learned in the tradition of the old apprenticeship in the different trades. The discovery and identification of the intrapsychic life of the subject, which linked with a chain of philosophical works on the nature of the human subject, provided few very precious understandings and explanations of the duality of the conscious-unconscious. Thus, psychoanalysis has to be considered an extension of many intellectual activities that preceded it, which have previously made the human subject its subject matter (Laplanche, 1997). Those prior efforts were by the philosophers and their works made it possible and useful to give psychoanalysis a new birth out of its limited definition as a psychotherapy.

The philosophical endeavors of the Western Culture, particularly since the seventeenth century, were advancing the concept of the human subject in parallel to the great achievements in the fields of physical sciences (Nomothetic sciences). The philosophers' incremental uncovering of the characteristics of what is human in the human subject got them nearer to the conception of the unconscious. Few of them literary mentioned it and should not be denied some claim to paving the way for Freud and some of his followers to discovering it. The unconscious – as we later found out – is entwined with consciousness and needed to be deciphered to bring it out as a separate stipulation. This was not possible until it became clear from the psychoanalytic discovery that what we constantly do in approaching the phenomenon of the subject is *interpretative* work. The human phenomena proved to be an inscription of the subject that require interpretation. The notion of the duality of consciousness, which was expressed in the philosophers' discoveries as a complexity of the human phenomenon, seemed to embody a major breakthrough in the theory of the subject. Consciousness was no longer an epistemological entity, and psychoanalysis was a promising novelty that works on finding the source of that complexity, which eluded philosophy all that time.

Freud's addition to the philosophical accomplishments was the unveiling of the unconscious's linkage with discoveries of the intrapsychic life of the subject. He seems to have gotten the lead from the French schools of psychiatry that introduced the idea of 'splitting of consciousness.' The splitting of consciousness has shown that the subject has two parallel psychological lives of which only one he is unaware of. This new and proven fact through hypnosis promised an explanation of both the impurity and complexity of consciousness. Freud was able to make that discovery a first step in understanding a myriad of other psychical phenomena. He led a movement that – unintentionally – instituted psychoanalysis as a *structural* theory of the subject. Gradually, he instated a methodology of exploring that field. For reasons that are beyond the bounds of this book, *the methodology of exploring the subject surpassed the theoretical aspects of the discovery.*

There are several significant features in the evolution of discovering the subject, which suggest an unconscious inclination in humanity to that discovery i.e., discovering itself. I am not using the term 'unconscious' here in its common psychoanalytic meaning of the repressed; I am using it to mean an almost uncanny and spontaneous inclination to surprisingly 'find out.' This feature is intrinsic in any structural theorizing, because revealing the structural nature of the subject of attention is never happened by planning. Reviewing the works of the thinkers and the philosophers who contributed to that evolution reveals a specific trend to build on the previous efforts in a seemingly organized and systematic way, yet it is done unconsciously or unintentionally. The works of the philosophers before Freud's discovery was not intentionally advancing toward creating psychoanalysis, but it cleared the view for Freud to see what to discover next. The psychoanalytic discoveries in themselves are gradual, unintended insights of the most particular and peculiar of the human subject. It would be no surprise if we discover in the history of psychoanalysis itself something similar to what we could mention about philosophical evolution.

Freud's work was a sequence of discoveries in the clinical field and in some interesting related areas of human activity. His accomplishments were made in steps followed by theoretical formulations. Thus, psychoanalysis was always 'work in progress' despite Freud's several attempts at considering his latest theoretical formulation a final statement about the psychical life of the subject. In other terms, during Freud's life there was no final theoretical formulation of his views, and psychoanalysis did not have one theory that could get the approval of all analysts. Psychoanalysts get bemused when asked about the theory of psychoanalysis, because they still do not have one. Psychoanalysis had a theoretical jolt in the late sixties and the early seventies when structuralism was introduced to it by Lacan and several thinkers who were active in their own fields of interest (see, E. Kurzweil, 1980). Instead, the new notion of structuralism created splits and acrimonies. Point in fact, psychoanalysts (including the Lacanians) and the IPA organizations are interested in psychoanalysis as much as it is divisions and conflicts. They turned the chance to give structuralism their attention to an occasion for posturing and upstaging.

Structuralism put psychoanalysis in quite a different and novel perspective. The birth of 'structuralism' and the resistance of functional thinking to subside made it inevitable for psychoanalysis to fragment into schools. Structuralism heightened the flaws of functional psychoanalytic thinking that dominated the classical theory, thus there was confusion about how to deal with that alarming threat to the old. The regular clinical psychoanalysts were aware of those flaws that limited their clinical effectiveness, but because of their professional background and nature of their training they were not able to follow the structural revolution. Instead, they tried creating their own functional theories. The problem with that movement is the way they dealt with the most basic and fundamental of the psychoanalytic discovery: the intrapsychic. A new plea to change the focus of analysis from the intrapsychic to relationality pervaded. Relational psychoanalysis became the response to structuralism[3].

Their attempts were creating new functional theories. Those theories (schools) were and are still unsuccessful, because the solution of the crisis was abandoning functionalism and adopting structuralism, not create 'other' functional theories. A move or a change of that nature existed in particular in France (Lacan, Laplanche, Green, supported by works from Derrida, Ricoeur, Foucault). The difference is fundamental because a school of psychoanalysis claims the right to make corrections presumed to be in the classical theory of psychoanalysis. Accordingly, it could replace the classical theory, not only improve it. The difference is clearer in comparing the Kleinian object-relations theory and Mitchell's relational psychology. What transpired from those attempts was several replacement versions of the classical theory that were sometimes quite opposed to the basics of the classical theory.

Is psychoanalysis a theory or has interpretations of issues regarding the subject?

Psychoanalysts have problems settling on a clear identification of what they work with, what they work for, and what their work accomplishes or should accomplish. The reason is lack of distinction between psychoanalysis as a theory of a 'subject matter,' and being a specific approach of studying different issues; like the difference between 'a theory of morality' and a moralistic theory of issues. The absence of that distinction comes from the absence of a definite identification of the subject matter of psychoanalysis. The reason is that psychoanalysis – as agreed upon – is a product of Freud's clinical work. His main concern in his clinical work was the split of consciousness and the formation of the unconscious. This remained the central idea in the theory of psychoanalysis, which remained sort of a theory of psychopathology. His work as a physician was about the 'patient' or the human subject when he gets psychologically affected. Therefore, psychoanalysis started as a clinical discipline. However, Freud's clinical writings are fewer and less impressive compared with the rest of his other works. Therefore, it is not easy to define the subject matter of psychoanalysis: is it the patient or is it the subject that could become a patient?

The theoretical part of Freud's work is where we can follow his evolving thought and the birth of his intuitions, if we approach it scholarly. Freud started developing his theoretical work by an interest in some common, if not even

---

[3] Most relational psychoanalysts consider Klein's theory the onset of relational psychoanalysis. Klein's work is about the effect of the early relations on the structuring of the child's intra-physical system.

banal, psychological aspects of the individual. He wrote three early works on dreams (1900a), parapraxes (1901b), and jokes (1905c), Freud's analysis of those three issues indicates that he has chosen them deliberately to reveal his intuition that psychical phenomena, even in the normal conditions of the subject are meaningful expressions of something latent. They are manifestation of something that is not fully understandable. A dream is a psychical event that happens while the subject is not fully conscious therefore it needs interpretation. A slip of the tongue could express the opposite of the speaker's intention or refer to something else in a vague way. Interpretation is again required. A joke or a funny situation is most of the time revealing two completely different intentions and is as such an unexpected interpretation in its own right. The three psychological events find their way to consciousness through some psychological processing. His pioneering theoretical work was intuitively structuralist, which suggests that Freud was ahead of his time in that respect. He concluded, for example, that the structure of the dream is a fulfilled wish, and a parapraxis structured by two conflicting but overlapping intentions in the same slip, and that a joke manages to conceal an objectionable viewpoint within a simple honest plain statement. He went further to discover the versatility of the structure the conscious-unconscious in all psychic phenomena.

The second point to highlight is the manner those discoveries in the daily attributes of the subject were in actuality advancing the clinical aspect of psychoanalysis. As Freud was able to read in a dream a hidden fulfilled wish, he was able to hear and see in the patients' associations and symptoms something said in disguise. He established that the subject shows and displays within what is manifest something latent. Moreover, he demonstrated that all conscious (manifest) features in the subject incorporate something unconsciously latent. *Freud underlined and demonstrated a 'basic' duality in the nature in the human subject.* The subject's duality required interpretation to be comprehended. Symptoms like dreams, as well as jokes and parapraxes, are the manifest of some things latent and the link between them is interpretative, i.e., the human phenomenon is always structural and subject to interpretation. This view point made a theory of the subject easier to reach. In previous attempts at understanding the nature of the human subject it was thought that there are two separate lines to follow: one for normal matters and one for abnormal or pathological matters. Freud showed and proved that the subject, regardless of his condition, is one and the same entity; but is a duality. The subject matter of psychoanalysis is the subject in whatever capacity he is, i.e., patient, artist, psychoanalyst, etc.

Starting psychoanalysis with the three early structural books obliged paying attention to two fundamental psychoanalytic ideas. Firstly, the psychical manifestation of the subject, healthy or sick, is always the synthesis of two coexisting elements that are usually antithetical. The second is that the link between what is manifested and its latent content is always unconscious. Understanding a psychological event fully depends on deducing that link from what is conscious. He even went further. Quite early in his discovery, as we will see later, he believed that understanding anything psychopathological will basically come from understanding the phenomena in its normal state. In other terms, Freud was aspiring to get to a theory of what could expose the natural processes that create the natural reactions in the normal, natural subject. Matter of fact, in hindsight, this very early notion could make us think that Freud sought after a theory of the subject to build upon it a structural view of psychopathology. His correspondence with Fleiss (Masson, 1989) reveals his dormant aspiration to formulate a theory that would make his views on psychopathology stand on the firm basis of the psychology of the normal subject. He aspired to know how things work naturally to explain better what and how things could go wrong.

Psychoanalysts rarely acknowledge that they have no conception of psychological health to be able to make the distinction between the sick and the healthy subjects. This is a major disadvantage for the clinical psychoanalyst, because a veritable theory of psychopathology cannot stand on its own without good complimentary theory of psychical normality, i.e., a theory of the subject. The issue of talking about the subject in his two capacities of patient and just a natural person is essential in advancing psychoanalysis beyond its present stagnation. A theory of the subject would have been impossible to think of before the birth of structuralism, because considering the 'intrapsychic' a structural foundation of the human phenomena required that Freud would have a good grasp of philosophy, and that his psychoanalysis is a theory of something(s) and not a theory in its own right yet. He might have also lacked the philosophical background needed for just entertaining a nonfunctional explication of psychic phenomena.

Psychoanalysis: Learning or Training?

A theory of the subject would reveal the need for a different system of learning and training in psychoanalysis. It will also place it among the other human sciences that were based on the same idea of the subject. This way, psychoanalysis gets ideas from outside its limited sphere. Turning psychoanalysis into a human science makes its proper place to learn and get training in its widening scope of interests become academia. Moving the formation of analysts from the IPA institutes to university is a major and significant change. The present system of learning and training follows the old traditional middle-age model of trades, where learning was transmitting the knowledge and experience of a master tradesman directly to a new generation of pupils. This primitive way of learning was replaced by academic learning in all the known professions of the present time. A theory of the subject is essential to the life of psychoanalysis in the same way physiology is the foundation of internal medicine, and it would give psychoanalysis its true identity as a human science. This could only be done in the academic system of education as it is also impossible to come close to its higher standards in the system of the training adopted in the institutes that the IPA. In academia, learning and training will have to be fulltime, leveled according to its advancement, and gets linked with all the other flourishing humanities (Fayek, 2015). This change would face resistance from the IPA and from the psychoanalysts themselves. The IPA would lose its authority and privilege of accrediting training and certifying psychoanalysts. Psychoanalysts convinced themselves that they are an independent, self-sustaining, self-regulating discipline, and internationally organized. They convinced themselves too that they have a privileged status as a special breed of professionals who control all their affairs: selection, training, standards of qualifying, and certifying the graduates. However, the lack of the public's concern or attention to those self-made convictions tells us why we have the crisis mentioned above. Continuing to exist in our own cocoon and to self-deceive of being special resulted in all the implied defects in psychoanalysis: its deterioration as a service and profession, the decline of the competence of its practitioners, isolation from the main stream of health services, and the loss of a sense of worth.

On the other hand, if psychoanalysis becomes a theory of the subjective, it will gain the respectable status of a constituent of an academic entity. As such, it will comprise several specialties; one of them is psychotherapy, because the human subject can be the patient as well as many other entities. That will break the taboo of the tripartite system of training. Several human sciences will then contribute to that theory of the subject and will have much to say about its subject matter. Those changes will impact the current system of training, which has to take in consideration that it has to create a new concept of pathology that complements its theory of the human subject.

Chapter Two

Psychoanalysis: The Issue of Its Subject Matter

It might sound strange, if not unacceptable, to say that psychoanalysis did not and still does not have a recognizable subject matter that defines it. However, this is a fact because psychoanalysis in its functional form, which still pervades it, could be preoccupied with causal relations in psychical events, like repression generating phantasies (or the opposite). This is different from structural psychoanalysis that has not dug deep roots yet in the psychoanalytic circle with the same degree of dedication. Structuralism hones in on the subject matter of the phenomena that it deals with, like looking at dreams as states of wishing that bring past and present frustrations into dynamic duality that allows their unconscious fantasmic gratification. The difference between psychoanalysis of causal relations and psychoanalysis of subject matters is like the difference between causal theories of morality and a theory of morality.

Freud spent his life trying to give his discoveries the form of a comprehensive theory of the psyche. He kept changing and trying new angles but was not satisfied enough with any of the attempts to settle on one. One obvious thing that transpired in his attempts is the ambition to get a comprehensive functional theory that could give psychoanalysis the status of a nomothetic science, i.e., the sciences of causes and effect. The problem – as we will see later – was the resolve to find the psychical process that could explain all psychopathological processes and provide a cause to all its possible effects. Freud was dealing with phenomena, such as dreams and wish fulfilment and conversion hysteria and the problems of sexual conflicts, and so on, which were too complex to have a simple explanation of their causes. He tried to give a functional quality to the link between what he discovered in consciousness and what was unconsciously associated with what is discovered. That was an unrealistic aspiration because the factors creating a dream for instance are – on the one hand – different enough to create similar dreams in different people. On the other hand, are not repeatable even in the same person.

However, he managed to conclude, with some clinical evidence, that consciousness in hysteria links with some undesirable thoughts, and some of the affective concomitants of those thoughts find an outlet in the symptoms. Those findings let him formulate the theory of catharsis. It was his first theory that looked as if his findings could be put in a comprehensive causative format. This theory was followed by the more comprehensive formulation of the topographic conception of the psychical system, though the catharsis theory remained the operational theory in psychotherapy.

In later part of his life Freud came up with the 'structural' conception of the psychical system (1923b), and with various modifications to the concept of unconscious (see chapter seven). He also tried to combine the topographic point of view with the structural conception of the psyche in a metapsychology that could benefit from both points of view. He hoped that this last attempt at theorizing psychoanalytic discoveries will cover most or all the psychoanalytic issues in a functional manner. This attempt engendered a more complicated functional theory of the psychological life.

Theoretical endeavors in psychoanalysis remain aimed at getting functional explanations for psychical material. Not considering that any psychical phenomenon is the product of two distinctly different psychical systems should have discouraged psychoanalysts from maintaining functionalism in theorizing. The link between the conscious and its unconscious correspondent is not functional, because consciousness and unconsciousness are qualitatively different in all aspects; thus, one cannot be the cause of the other[1]. Consciousness could engender other similarly conscious material, as is the case with the unconscious. There is another problem with functional theories of psychoanalysis. Psychoanalysis is a discipline of the two related entities of psychopathology and psychotherapy. Although they link, it is not some simple link. Analysts turned the discoveries of psychoanalysis as whole into a theory of psychopathology, confusing theories of practice and theories of the subject matter of psychoanalysis. As they continued on in that vein, the contemporary theories of psychoanalysis proved unable to produce any theory that goes beyond the clinical life of the patient. The contemporary relational theories have almost nothing

---

[1] The onset of psychoanalysis was – and still is – based on the notion that the unconscious is secondary to consciousness, and more or less interferes with its functions. The unconscious is a basic mental, cognitive, affective condition in the human subject. Consciousness is a dormant potential. It evolves with growing up to replace the unconscious.

psychoanalytic to say about the personal, social, creative, political life of the *person*.

A Brief Account of Misguided Efforts

What is the course of development of the theory of psychoanalysis that eluded Freud and some of his early talented disciples? Freud's first attempt to form a psychological theory was based on the catharsis of the repressed, which started earlier in the phase of hypnosis. Then, his work on dreams revealed that the split of conscious-unconscious is not comprehensive enough to account for all that is involved in the studied phenomena. He noticed that the day residues that initiate the dream are states between consciousness and unconsciousness, i.e., precociousness. So, he construed a topographic model of the psyche, following his theory on dreams and expanded discoveries of the unconscious. Freud went back to the issue of sexuality as the main culprit in psychoneuroses, but this time and introduced the theory of the *Trieb* (1905c). The theory of infantile sexuality heralded the birth of the dynamic point of view a major change in the theory of the libido. He got the notion of libidinal regression to be invested in the subject and faced the issues of narcissism. After the papers of 'metapsychology papers' (1915c, d, e) he tried metapsychology as a theoretical framework. His concise definition of metapsychology (1940a) was not enough to allow it to become the basis of a general theory. Metapsychology was a simple usage of three qualitative aspects in psychical activity: the topographic, dynamics, and economics. Those three aspects of the psychic seemed able to account for the complexities of the psychical processes.

The discoveries in the intrapsychic life of the subject were increasing beyond Freud and his colleagues' ability to contain them in simple metapsychological formats. His last metapsychology, usually called, mistakenly, the structural point of view, was nothing more than the reification of elements of the intrapsychic. The creation of a quasi-psychology that was neither comprehensive to account for the richness of the intrapsychic life, nor had a clear place for the complex concept of the unconscious (see chapter seven) did not solve the problem of the subject matter of a theory of psychoanalysis. The structural metapsychology and its offshoot of ego psychology created a very peculiar situation in the history of the theory of psychoanalysis.

Freud's 'structural' metapsychology – as his last theoretical endeavor – looked as if it is the final stop in the psychoanalytic journey. Ego psychologists, especially in the USA, embarked on developing this point view as the classical and final theory. It took little time to realize its shortcomings, which came from being a theory of 'agencies' or psychological *things*. The tripartite division of the three agencies got psychoanalysis deeper in the limited functional point f view. The dissatisfaction with a stale theory of psychoanalysis revived the old disagreements of the very early conflicts in the IPA. The efforts of the IPA to contain those disagreements and the echoes of the splits in England, France, and seemingly the USA too resulted in call to accept what was called 'plurality of psychoanalysis' (Wallerstein, 1998). Psychoanalytic plurality as a plea did nothing more than offering different versions of functional psychoanalysis as better substitutes for the original one. In England and France there were attempts at interpreting Freud's thought, not just his works or words. Thus, ego psychology was sometimes unceremoniously dismissed. Rereading the *Freudian Text* scholarly offered better and more comprehensive understanding of psychoanalysis, most of the time rather free from the letter of the initial discovery.

A follower of the history of the theory would be overwhelmed when he reaches the seventies and the eighties of the last century. The field of psychoanalysis was bustling with theoretical 'offerings' with no noticeable presence of the original Freudian formulations. However, three main so-called schools came out as the most attractive to psychoanalysts: neo-ego psychology, the Kleinian (with several additions to its main premise of object relation), and the Lacanian (with great effort from its followers to keep it anchored in psychoanalysis). Those three main psychoanalytic streams showed, from the beginning, the signs of being stopgaps in a strong movement to replace the classical theory. The reason is now evident and understandable. Psychoanalysis – or the knowledge about the subject – outgrew the training system of the IPA institutes. In spite of the absence of a clear theory about the subject, still the new schools maintained their claim of their psychoanalytic origin and nature. The new theories did not have what it takes to declare their true metal; therefore, they stayed under the umbrella of psychoanalysis until their future would be tested. They were stopgaps in a movement that was directionless, but has the reputation of being the base of all schools.

Psychoanalysis suffered and still suffers from confusing the idea of a theory that has a subject matter and a theory that has only a method of practice. This confusion might be hiding within another between learning about the subject that the theory claims to represent and the training it offers to practice therapy on a subject we know very little about. Psychoanalysis is still learned in training institutes, where the distinction between those two sides is inadequately defined, if at all. The distinction between theory and practice was not a consideration in the early days of the movement because Freud's work did not give the impression that he had that distinction in mind. Continuing learning psychoanalysis in training institutions maintained, reinforced, and encouraged that fusion and protected it. As an example, the works of Bion (1965), Brenner's (1982) Laplanche (1989), were expositions of the core of the psychoanalytic theory, and also general theories of practice. They were not tentative attempts when they were originally initiated and were the thing needed to know. However, we cannot take them anymore in the same way. Psychoanalysis nowadays is clearly without a clear theory, even without an acceptable protocol of practice, since Freud's protocol is not followed anymore. We cannot even put those efforts in the same framework as a progressing psychoanalysis.

Psychoanalysis was the first and most ingenious exposition of the intrapsychic life of the person, which is not only the core of the human subject but is also what characterizes him as a special ontological entity. Nevertheless, it stopped short of declaring the human subject to be its subject matter. Freud and his colleagues were captives of their initial success in their clinical work; they did not pay attention to the subject behind the patients they had discovered and brought out of obscurity. The result is the present stagnation of the theory of psychoanalysis. However, psychoanalysis has already accumulated a rich literature about the human phenomena and its findings have found their way to the humanities and to social life in general, implying that psychoanalysis would not just disappear if the profession of psychoanalysis disappears.

Although several other human sciences have acknowledged the human subject as their subject matter, they seem to struggle with a missing part in their conception of the subject, which is essential in leading to a finality in the matters they study. Psychoanalysis has the most central piece in that puzzle: *the unconscious*. Laplanche asserted that the Western Culture is the culture of the *subject* (1992), yet, that culture still awaits psychoanalysis to give the final statement about the unconscious. It is very true that Western Culture in almost all its aspects is focused on the subject compared with the previous and different cultures. Yet, neither psychoanalysis is able to give the true conclusion for that issue nor the rest of the idiographic sciences are able to continue without the input from psychoanalysis. The problem is that the subject is a novel philosophical entity that is a recent issue which emerged lately from within structuralism.

The Gradual Birth of the Subject

The subject is an ontological entity that took thousands of years to gradually emerge from its original place in the world of animal beings to *be* and make *being* that psychological life we are examining in psychoanalysis.

The term 'subject' signifies consciousness and the consciousness of consciousness. Psychoanalysis is the science of that phenomenon which is the subject matter of its theory. In spite of the appearance of homosapiens few hundred thousand years ago, the 'human subject' is a novelty, in world of thinking, that can barely go back four or five decades. The beginning is not distant from the present status as might seem. It started as what is called 'the cognitive revolution' some seventy thousand years ago (Harari, 2016) when homosapiens paid attention to the world around them and realized that they need to explain everything in it, not just live in it like other creatures do. There was a gradual, yet fast, attention that things in the material world have meaning and finding meanings creates awareness and consciousness. This advancement changed the life of homosapiens. They sensed separateness from the material world around them and noticed their difference from the rest of beings. This change extended awareness to become a need for knowing. They gradually realized that they should ask about the world because they are the ones who should answer their own questions. The accumulation of answers and the inconsistencies in those answers from people to people, and from times to other times created curiosity about their own nature. It was new to make themselves subjects for examination, because understanding the world was dependent on their skills to get the causes and meaning of things, while knowing about the self was less clear. The way knowledge about the self was gathered was the topic of fascination, and also strife. It is important to underline that the emergence of the subject's sense of being within the development of the human race was subsequent to making some sense of the world around him. Their curiosity about their self underwent major transformations when some of them claimed to know more of what the others know because that was not an issue in knowing the material world around them.

The importance of underlining this fact lies in the heart of the difficulties homosapiens encountered in trying to understand themselves; a difficulty that persists till now. Learning about external reality is a cognitive process. Learning about one's self is a function of *intuition*, because man had to find some things tangible enough that could *reflect* his attributes to him first. After recognizing himself cognitively in that reflection first he had to secondly accept what he sees as his-self intuitively. This process produced a very sophisticated human phenomenon: mythology. After few centuries of animism, i.e., that everything around him was alive and has a spirit, the subject inserted himself in the world of the spirits and made up the stories which he became part of. Some of those myths taught the subject very novel things about himself and the forces he was entangled with (though he unconsciously

31

created). The subject treated mythical tales as historical facts without showing any attempt at questioning or explaining them.

After centuries of being stuck using animism and mythological thinking to get closer to understanding himself came a thinker (in the western hemisphere) who posited the first question for the subject to reflect upon himself. *Thales Meletus* (5th–4th BC), a pre-Socratic Greek thinker of Turkish residence, quizzed about how could he be sure that an idea that comes to his mind or told to him is true, correct, or wrong and untrue? How to examine ideas to be sure that they are true knowledge? This was the first time the *subject* faced himself as an ontological entity: asking himself questions that only he has the means and the responsibility to answer. *Thales'* query made Greek thinkers embark on the most exciting voyage of exploring the world of the subject, i.e., the things that puzzles him about himself, and the mental tools he uses in order to deal with that puzzlement. This way, the subject became the issue of philosophical thought, and remained ever since. The human subject lost his awe of things by knowing that he can be certain about his judgment, as *Thales* has pointed out. However, this distinct knowledge was very gradual and, interestingly, looks as if it was unintentional. Nevertheless, something about its evolution forces the impression that it has been unconsciously predetermined.

Before moving to what Greek philosophy did to the subject, it is important to keep in mind a question the answer of which is the basis of all the failed attempts at building functional theories in the humanities: how to distinguish between what is cause and what is the effect in human phenomena? Did the subject change to move from mythology to philosophy or did philosophy change his views of mythology? I am posing this question to underline that the change in the place the subject occupied in the theory of knowledge, which Thales started, is a typical dialectical interaction that is the nature of the human sciences. Some change preceded Thales' question for it to become the instrument of the change he initiated. This is not the case in the nomothetic sciences, because their subject matters do not get engaged with the thinker or participates in any interaction (see chapter ten). The subject of the fifth century BC either got involved in the radical change of defining himself because of philosophical thinking, or coincidentally gave birth to philosophy and take over that task.

Myths developed as local creations that pertain to local histories. With time and immigration of people they overlapped and fused in a process of mutual insemination. The expanding world of the subject needed more encompassing and general myths and less specific characterization of the main parties involved in the stories. Hence, religions were born. Religions were advancements to mythologies because they addressed a main and most cardinal structure in the life of the subject: the issue of origins (Christian, 2018). *What is the origin of the world and of us?* In the same way the subject created myths and believed them as history, he also created religions and believed they were *delivered* to answer the question of origins. He accepted to alienate from himself by not acknowledging that he created what tells him about his creation. The most peculiar about this process is its 'persistence' and its impact on the subject's sense of being, and the additional change it made to it. The subject embarked on a trip of defining himself through the logic of (his) religion. Although the subject 'played it as it goes,' the outcome, retrospectively speaking, looks as if the subject was unconsciously decided about what he aims at. The human subject's sense of being emerged as an immediate response to a strong anxiety about the correctness of his self-awareness. Religious fanaticism and religious wars expressed *his* anxiety about his beliefs in the form of aggression towards who do not accept his dogma. After a very abrupt decline of the religion of Mount Olympia, Greek mythology turned the corner to become Greek philosophy. In spite of the prevalence of religion for few centuries the human subject ultimately submitted it to the philosophical standers of discussions of everything else. The tradition of Greek mythology did not distract the philosopher from seeing the other side of the subject: the non-mythical side.

Thinkers and philosophers put aside his mythological heritage and became more interested in knowing about the phenomenon of the subject himself. They noted that the subject thinks, feels, changes, evolves, relates, and is capable sometimes of taking himself as an object of curiosity. Greek philosophers, and Aristotle in particular, offered descriptions, explanations, observations, and opinions of all those attributes of the subject, even of the material world around him. Those philosophical endeavors replaced the religious heritage of explanation to the extent that when the contemporary world of religions appeared the Greek heritage became the foundation of the Christian church's dogma.

At this point we can see that the subject has emerged from the cognitive revolution of seventy thousand years ago as the main subject of curiosity and the most difficult problem to solve. *He is the thing to know and the one to do the knowing.* This way, a branch of knowledge was born and a specialty was created: pure philosophy. The emergence of the subject is the emergence of pure philosophy as the subject's venture to understand. We can now advance to study and scrutinize what philosophy did to the concept of the subject.

The Subject in Philosophy

The link between philosophy and the subject is not functional or that one is the result of the other. Philosophy is the fabric of civilization and Greek philosophy is the early threads of western civilization. At its beginning, it dealt with what preoccupied the subject in regard to nature and his place in it. By the time it was fading out, its great philosophers left us a great number of modalities of thinking about things. Aristotle was encyclopedic enough to add most of what have been said about the material world of the subject. The birth of Christianity put the subject in a very different and puzzling context: thinking and believing. Christianity came up with a book (the Bible) that had readymade formulations of the issues' origins, ethics, and truth, etc. However, the most serious issue in that stand was the demand that the subject revokes reasoning matters and accepts only what is delivered to him by faith. It looks that Christianity was a major blow to philosophy or it was itself a warped philosophy. It was, in hindsight, a progress in the walk of the subject toward a true consciousness (true consciousness is consciousness of consciousness). Two things came out of Christian philosophy, if we could call it so. The first is the subject gaining – consciously – an identity that defines him. His identity, which comes from belonging to a church made him aware of the other 'subjects,' who have different religions or identities. The second gain was awareness of the factor of intentionality in deciding about one's identity. Although faith was stealing the subject's freedom of choice his faith eluded him, and he believed in freedom of choosing his identity. Christian thought became the philosophy that took the empty place mythology left by the end of Greek philosophy.

It was predictable that the conflict between faith and thinking will eventually make philosophy stand against stopping the advancement toward freeing the subject so he could find himself at the end. So, the church tried to philosophize its dogma by creating sort of rapprochement with philosophy. It considered theology a religious arena for philosophers to try their thinking. Beside that significant change in the life of the subject, the social and economic developments in Europe added more and very complex field of subjective identifications, like class identification. The subject was defined by his faith, but now he could be defined by his trade and social class too. It is not enough for the subject to be a Christian Catholic; he also had the identity of his social class (serf or land owner) working the land or administering the surfs that do that.

Philosophy reacted to those changes in the world of the subject. In a relatively short time – around the seventh century AD – education and seminaries turned philosophy into a profession in its own right. The importance of that change is that philosophers studied the subject as a *subject matter* of their philosophical work. The subject was no longer merely a topic in philosophy; he became the subject matter of philosophy itself. The subject was the center of attention in what is named scholastic philosophy, or the phase of scholasticism. The philosophers from the twelfth century to the seventeenth century were distinctly dedicated to knowing the subject as a thinking learning subject. They itemized thinking and studied those items extensively. Their findings were a source of great understanding of *how* the subject perceives the world and understands it. They established that thinking as a process does not happen haphazardly and were able to fascinate the subject by showing how his mind works to know. Scholastics immersed themselves in studying the subject's knowledge and thinking processes, and they accumulated a great deal of knowledge about the two sides of the gap that *Thales* highlighted.

They made great strides in knowing about knowing, better, about the subject's mind more than about the subject as such. They were lagging in the area of knowing the knower, i.e., the subject who does the knowing or the knowing subject in all of that. It was like asking the question: now we know how we think about things, and we know what we thought about those things, but we do not know if what we called thinking is really thinking or – for instance – perception or memory? Thinking about thinking had to wait till the seventeenth century to gradually occupy the core of philosophy, and even gives it a second start after *Thales* made the first start with Aristotle perfecting it.

The second start was René Descartes's making. He asked the question *Thales* asked before in 1637, but he started a theory related to the subject, not to the objects of the subject was querying about[2]. He took the stand that the important issue is *certainty is in regard to the subject not the objects.* Thus, the proof of the subject's existence is the issue and guarantees that we could fall back to it to ascertain the existence of everything else. 'I have to prove that I existed first before questioning the existence of everything else.' The answer was deceptively simple: *I think, therefore I am,* a statement dubbed 'the Cartesian Cogito.' The Cartesian notion was that the subject's mere doubts and uncertainties attest to his existence through whatever he concluded about matters. Since the *Cogito*, the subject who was always considered an ontological entity that could be turned into an item for study like everything proved to be – and fundamentally – a duality within that entity: *a thinker and a thinker of his thinking, a doubter of his doubts.* The duality of the subject like

---

[2] Thales question was regarding the object of thinking. Descartes question was regarding the thinker.

feeling and feeling of feelings, consciousness and conscious of consciousness, etc. directed the philosophers to study the subject and his duality instead of the old duality of the subject versus the world. In the two centuries after Descartes, philosophers explored the subject's dual existence as the main philosophical issue and exposed a basic characteristic in it: *the human mind is not the seat of unitary processes of mentation but a generator of dualities that affects his being as a subject.* Better, the subject's duality reflects the subject's proclivity to respond to the world and even to himself by dividing matters into opposites: manifest qualities and latent content or meaning (will get to that later). After long and remarkable explorations in the subject's mind (self!) by great thinkers, their efforts came to an impasse: what is the nature and characteristic of the 'links between the created opposites in those dualities? If the subject is incapable of thinking in a unitary way of the world, and his mind creates a *subjective* duo of every *objective* notion, then what is the nature of the link between the subjective *I* and the objective *me*?'

It became clear that the subject's being is – intrinsically – a merger or a duality of objective (manifest) and subjective (meaning, or latent). The philosophical impasse regarding the links within those dualities needed a solution. Psychoanalysis, and more precisely Freud, came with a conception of the link that was portending a solution. As we could see from Freud's correspondence (Masson, 1985), he was aspiring for his work with patients to get him to a theory of the nature of the human subject. Implicit in that aspiration is awareness that psychoanalysis is not just psychotherapy or a theory of psychopathology. His ambition to understand and theorize about the subject's normal states attest to the fact that *we psychoanalysts could not be in full command of our therapeutic work if we do not have a definition of normality or health.*

Ironically, Freud's work on non-psychopathological issues (human phenomena like dreams, religion, etc.) is the source of the fundamentals of psychoanalysis as left it to us and is the core of a theory of the subject. Freud did not notice till the end that his solution to the problem of the theory of subject is already there and was unconsciously forming it all along. Although none of Freud's attempts at formulating a comprehensive theory of the subject has been final, sufficient, or convincing, there is no doubt that any possible theory of the subject has to be traced back to Freud's psychoanalytic discoveries. Nevertheless, doing that requires new reframing of the psychoanalytic discoveries to consider them the basics of a theory of the subject.

The Need for a Theory of the Subject

It is expected that the idea of a need for a theory of the subject will raise several conflicting responses. The clinical psychoanalysts would say that such theory has no practical usefulness to their practice. Other theorists in the humanities might claim that they already have one, which even includes aspects of the theory of unconscious; therefore, they do not need such a theory. Some might ask whether we need one theory of the subject or several theories. Others would wonder what does psychoanalysis have to do with such a theory, and that it should be left to philosophy to initiate? A few might advocate keeping this theory the ambition of several idiographic sciences because it relates to the problem of multiple issues that do not pertain to one aspect of the subject?

As I mentioned above, we still do not have a comprehensive theory of psychoanalysis itself. We only have few quasi-theories regarding issues we encounter in the psychopathology of the patients, or encounter in a general discussion about some problems of practice. A theory is a statement or several statements on the structure of a subject, the functions of that structure, and the workings that keep the structure and its functions compatible. To have a theory of psychoanalysis we need to identify its subject matter; its structure and the functions of that structure, and then review and revise our conception of the applications of that theory in what looks relevant to its core. We should also show how the structure of its subject matter engenders its functions.

We hardly find in the contemporary schools of psychoanalysis, which are mixtures of notions regarding psychopathology and psychotherapy, any shared identifiable subject matter. Stating the subject matters of those schools could be worked out to give those schools the legitimacy of a comprehensive theory of a kind. *Psychoanalysis cannot survive anymore without a comprehensive theory, which is better to be of the human subject.* The assumed theoretical body of psychoanalysis is so cluttered with the debris of the defunct schools that it is difficult to find a meaningful starting point in defining it. There was a period in the middle of the twentieth century when psychoanalysis had what looked like a subject matter, expressed in tendencies and efforts to expand psychoanalysis and deal with new forms of psychopathology (psychoses, psychosomatics, character formations, and widening the scope of its practice to include some social issues). Those expansions were not expanding psychoanalysis but only its sphere of practice, and at best just made psychoanalysis a better practice of psychotherapy, the search for a true subject matter made psychoanalysis go into a spiral of deterioration and loss of orientation. There were some attempts to take psychoanalysis out of the clinic to explore other areas of human activities like art and some social phenomena, but those attempts were so saturated with the ideas of psychopathology that they failed to catch the attention of the non-clinically oriented intellectuals.

There was a strong reluctance to look for a subject matter of psychoanalysis from outside the psychopathology field. It was also discouraging to think of defining a subject matter for psychoanalysis from the failings that started to plague its practice. Yet, there were short episodes and few acknowledged efforts to do so, though indirectly. Those attempts were characterized by works based on the assumption that the human subject was latent in every Freudian attempt to create a theory of psychoanalysis. Just to mention a few: the reconstitution of the psychosexual model of development (Erikson, 1950), Bouvet's weaving the object relational theory in the stages of development (1967), Bion's reading of the thinking process (1965, 1988), Green's expounding the issue of affect (1999c). Those were the closest psychoanalysis came to a theory of the subject. However, those attempts did not attract the attention of psychoanalysts because *a theory of the subject is about the subject before being run through their theory of psychopathology.* That was not available to Freud and consequently was not acceptable to the clinical psychoanalysts. There is still a stubborn attrite among analysts that the only approach, or the better approach, to the subject of psychoanalysis is the clinical approach. Psychoanalysis has to have a theory of the 'normal healthy' human subject if it could claim its confidence in talking about psychopathology. Better, psychoanalysis has to have a theory of normal psychical dynamics (the same as physiology and anatomy work for medicine[3]) if they want to talk with confidence of psychopathology. Analysts, especially those who openly advocate a certain theory like the Kleinians and the relationists, have sophisticated and elaborated language to talk about psychopathology, yet they cannot say much in the same language about the healthy psyche.

Configuring such a theory has to be the work of analysts from the different schools, so it will make sense in their endeavors. It might also save future psychoanalysis from new disintegration. Nevertheless, what is equally significant in configuring a theory of the subject is having a theory of practice

---

[3] The profession of the medicine-man existed, in one form or the other, for centuries before the birth of medicine in the mid nineteenth-century. The birth of medicine came about when some apprentices of the medicine-man looked differently at sicknesses to discover what went wrong in the healthy processes. The physician is the medicine man who knows what went wrong with the what and the how of the body.

that is a product of real understanding of what is done in psychotherapy. If we continue separating theory from practice in psychoanalysis in its general meaning, practice will continue to have no grounds to stand on, or a practice which has no specific quality to make of it a profession that could support its self. The importance of highlighting this point is clear in the clinical practice of psychoanalysis. Without a theory of a 'normal' subject, we should expect no real criteria for psychopathology, only made-up formulations of causes of psychopathology. When we psychoanalyze a patient with depression caused by childhood neglect, we could be making generalization that turns the patient into an object of childhood neglect. This attitude is a product of a theory of psychopathology and the absence of the theory of subject. This makes psychopathological theories merely points of view. Moreover, without a theory of the normal subject psychopathology will become merely irregularities in some of the subject's psychical functions when the subject *as whole* be experiencing his own painful childhood conditions. This is what is happening now and psychoanalysis is spiraling down both in credibility and in its efficacy as therapy.

At this point I would make a distinction that will be the core issue in this book: the subject matter of psychoanalysis is the intrapsychic structures[4] of the subject, which is his actual and factual self. From this angle of looking at things, *psychopathology is what happens to the formation and structure of the intrapsychic dynamics of the subject.* Therefore, a theory of the subject is a theory of the formation of the human intrapsychic. Psychoanalysts still believe that 'real' psychoanalysis was born in the *Clinique*, and its practice is the dealing with symptoms, dreams, transference resistances, etc. If we accept that psychoanalysis is just an act of psychotherapy, we would be denying it, and denying ourselves too, a remarkable history of our profession, and an equally remarkable link between psychoanalysis and other major cultural feats. The philosophical endeavors of the seventeenth and the eighteen centuries, in the German idealist philosophy in particular, paved the way for Freud and some of his followers to institute 'a' theory of the subject as a constituent of this western culture. Psychoanalysis is the latest and most noticeable attempt at discovering the nature of the human subject and formulating an inclusive theory about his nature. What is significant to note and study is the unintentional emergence of the concept of the unconscious among the philosophers who were studying the subject. When we look at it now, we cannot miss that it – the unconscious – is not a discovery; it is a recovery or

---

[4] This distinction is meant to underline that relational theories will not be considered in this book viable sources of a theory of the subject.

uncovering its cover. The same thing happened to Freud in a reverse way: he was studying the unconscious and unintentionally the 'subject' became the subject matter of psychoanalysis and Freud's claim to real fame is discovering for us the nature of consciousness.

The Intrapsychic and the Subject

The main psychoanalytic contribution to the philosophers' endeavors was identifying the psychical life of the subject and its characteristics as the core of a theory of the 'object.' The philosophers looked as if getting closer to defining the subject, but their approach was mainly pertaining to the issue of causality or explaining several observations about the subject. They were unable to get to the origins of any particular causality that is functioning in the subject. Freud and his disciples discovered the psychodynamics of the intrapsychic life of the subject. They uncovered the existence of a psychical life that is not available to observation without knowing the language it uses to express itself. This was the missing part in the puzzle that philosophy failed to deal with. *The human subject is not comprehensible without including his intrapsychic life* in any observation about him. The work of the philosophers, before Freud's discovery, was not intentionally meant to lead to the creation of psychoanalysis, but with no exaggeration, it was the logical precedence and the essential endeavor that affected its birth.

Whatever the psychoanalysts do to make psychoanalysis clear and definable, even to themselves, they face the problem of 'what' are they talking about: the patient or the human subject. The reason for suggesting this distinction is that psychoanalysis was born in two different areas at the same time, to the same father, Freud. Freud was exploring – by hypnosis – the etiology of hysteria and psychoneuroses in general, and forming some theoretical ideas about psychopathology. His main concern was the splitting of consciousness in psychopathology, which was the revolutionary discovery of French psychiatry. The symptom, thus, comprised unarticulated repressed material. His work as a physician was about the 'patient' or the human subject when he gets psychologically affected. Thus, one of two aspects of psychoanalysis was born in the *Clinique*. At that same time, Freud was exploring other human phenomena that normally pertain to customary psychological aspects of the subject and are unrelated to psychopathology: dreams, parapraxes, jokes, and some minor other psychosocial phenomena. He discovered in those 'normal' phenomena implicit facts. They proved that the subject's natural characteristics are manifestations of latent material and are complex expressions of that material. The psychical attributes within the manifest gave unexpected meaning to those manifest happenings, and another 'unspecific' line of exploration of the subject was born. Splitting of consciousness in itself – between the manifest and the latent – was the very nature of anything that could be called psychological. Although the two lines of interest seemed unrelated, they were preliminarily sharing something in common: the symptom and the dream were both the manifestation of some things latent, which the subject is unconscious of. *In the symptom (psychopathology) the latent is repressed, while in the conscious and natural psychical events (slip of the tongue) it is only distorted.* A theory of the subject would reveal that training in psychoanalysis has to change from training to learning; learning about the subject as a precondition for training to do therapy.

Those two observations look to us now so banal to mention, but they hold two basic and fundamental psychoanalytic ideas. Firstly, the psychical manifestations of the subject, healthy or sick, are always a synthesis of two opposing elements (theses). The second is about a link between the manifest component and its latent content. That link, in any psychical event, is always unconscious and a full understanding of psychological event is contingent on deducing it from what is analyzed. In other terms, Freud was very close to saying plainly that a theory of the human subject is the prerequisite for understanding psychopathology and it should be the structural theory of psychoanalysis. The problem of talking about the subject in his two capacities of patient and just normal and natural phenomenon did not, and still does not, get the desired attention from psychoanalysts.

What psychoanalysts talk about in regard to the subject and to the patient reveals an important issue. After all what is said and done, the theory of pathology is based on the notion of increases or decreases in certain healthy processes and functions. The affected processes neither have a proper definition to consider their healthy states, nor relate to the human condition in its natural state to entertain an explanation of its current condition. It seems that analysts have decided that psychological health is merely the absence of sickness. Could that principle apply to physical health and sickness? Could a physician say that this person is healthy because he is not sick?

A theory of the subject is the future of psychoanalysis because it is needed to stop psychoanalysis declining in quality, creating the crisis in its practice. The condition of the present systems of training in psychoanalysis has obvious negative effects on very weak and unguided attempts to develop a theory of the subject that would take psychoanalysis to wider horizons of the psyche. It is not improving teaching or replacing the dated theory with new findings. After decades of discussing, arguing, condemning, complaining of our system of training there is an unhealthy refusal to see and acknowledge that the current system of training needs, if not demand, a total review of its purpose. We should do what Eitingon himself did: build a training system that suits our time in regard to the psychoanalysis we have now and should have in the future.

What happens when the theory of the subject becomes the theory of psychoanalysis? The theory of the subject will expand the scope of studying and working with the subject, whether as a member of a group activity or the initiator of a group activity. The 'subject' transcends his individual status and presents analysts with a myriad of subjective events to deal with. Psychotherapy will be only one of several other needed areas of expertise. No institute training would be suitable for training in psychoanalysis if psychoanalysis is expanded to be a theory of the subject. Some aspects of training might still benefit from learning from the experienced analysts but that would be done in a different context. Several human sciences are needed to contribute to the theory of the subject and to be part of the learning material for the new psychoanalyst. Psychoanalysis will have to develop the various training methods that suit the various psychoanalytic specialties. Psychoanalysis is a science in its own right (see chapter ten) and will branch out into varied specialties. Thus, it will need input from several other human sciences, and will need more time to qualify its graduates. Therefore, it needs to be a full-fledged academic endeavor, with recognized levels of competence and specializations and higher levels of certifications.

Chapter Three
The Roots of Psychoanalysis in Philosophy

Psychoanalysts, generally speaking, are not interested in psychoanalysis outside its clinical context. They are neither cognizant nor mindful of the significance of knowing their cultural heritage. They learn psychoanalysis from mostly physicians or clinicians who – whatever their culture and erudition is – do not see psychoanalysis within a 'cultural context.' The present condition of psychoanalysis proposes that clinical psychoanalysts, who are still considered the only legitimated analysts, do not seem to find an appropriate context for 'their' psychoanalysis: *what and where does psychoanalysis generally belong in epistemology!* It is neither pure practice of body of knowledge like in medicine, nor a science in its own right like psychology. Psychoanalysts, without a grasp of their heritage and a clear vision of their proper place in the future of their culture will retain a parochial and archaic vision of themselves. This view is influenced by relating psychoanalysis, solely to the mental health profession. They will continue to believe that what they know of psychoanalysis (and keep teaching to new generations) is all of what psychoanalysis is about. A vision of that nature has negative impact on theoretical advancement and evolution, and is not conducive to prepare psychoanalysis to the demands of the changes that took place in the last half century and will take place in people and the society in the coming future. It will continue deteriorating because without a recognizable and a clear present no future could be envisaged.

There is a reason for analysts' reluctance to see psychoanalysis in a context different from the context of the mental health field and clinical practice. At the beginning, the psychoanalytic institution was keen to limit learning (training) psychoanalysis to people who are part of the mental health field, who were then mostly physicians. In hindsight, the organization had good reasons for that. Psychoanalyzing could have been taken up by people who are not qualified to see patients in the first place. However, something had to be decided from the beginning, yet was not: is there more to psychoanalysis than psychoanalyzing? If so (no major disagreements on that were raised even then and till now), how do we make the distinction between the different psychoanalyses and include the differences in learning and training? Because psychoanalysis was not recognized as a profession, and still it is not, it was risky to consider it in a non-medical context, especially that it was without the defining means of a clear identified theory. Freud and early analysts struggled with the issue of 'lay analysts' (Freud, 1926 e). Eventually this matter was settled in the courts. But the settlement was not about what is psychoanalysis; it was about who else than the physicians could see patients and practice psychoanalyzing. Settling the matter this way left the core problem unsettled till now. As long as psychoanalysis is viewed outside any historical context, it will remain a puzzle to everyone: is it knowledge that has a practical side? Or is it just a skill that requires training to improve it, or could it be something more general than what is perceived of it till now? Without realizing its origin, psychoanalysis will not have an answer to any of those questions.

The Search for an Origin for Psychoanalysis

Whenever the history of any major human endeavor is mentioned, we are reminded of Newton's famous saying: I only saw further because I stood on the shoulders of giants. Psychoanalysts do not realize or accept that psychoanalysis is a stage in a long history of thinking that was philosophical thinking, which preceded it and led to its birth. German ideal metaphysics is the immediate philosophical background of the modern age of philosophy. It was indirectly the point from which psychiatry in Europe emerged. This background is accountable for the profound characteristics of Western culture in general, because it impacted the general educational systems in Europe. Freud was educated in that system, which incorporated the contributions of those philosophical thought in its core curricula (Gymnasium). Therefore, despite Freud admitting that he intentionally avoided reading the works of some thinkers and philosophers to avoid being influenced by them, it was not possible to avoid their influence on his thinking completely (Roudinesco, 2016). He disregarded that we assimilate our cultures not cognitively but unconsciously. Whatever he did, did not immunize himself from the influence of those thinkers, who shaped the Western mind and all its cultural matters.

Most psychoanalysts would consider the effort to locate psychoanalysis within the Western Culture of little relevance to their work. This attitude is embedded in another more crucially misleading conviction: psychoanalysts – who are mental health practitioners by virtue of their academic background – they believe that they do not need to learn more than the psychoanalytic theory of psychopathology and the technicalities of practicing psychotherapy to qualify as psychoanalysts. Accordingly, psychoanalysis as psychotherapy is looked at as a self-contained entity. It could or should be learned in specialized institutes, and for the graduates to form closed communities of people of their kind. The once highly admired source of new discoveries in the field of the humanities became a discipline of recyclable knowledge. Although psychoanalysis is not suffering from this progressive condition equally in every part of the world, there is no denying, though, that it is happening universally and creating a global crisis. All the attempts at dealings with the crisis have failed, yet psychoanalysts and the psychoanalytic organizations still insist on repeating the same modality of training. The training modality has become: *keep the system as is but improve it.* Psychoanalysts proved their inability to think outside the limitations of training in the IPA institutes. They did not ponder that the system they adhere to is the cause of the crisis. Improving the system could only complicate matters more. It will accentuate its flaws and just tinkering with some of its details consequently will make it get more distorted.

Psychoanalysis is an expression of a whole culture that has more means of expressing itself than just psychoanalysis. If the idea is accepted, it will indicate that psychoanalysis still has an important place in the culture. Therefore, it is wrong to see it in isolation of its culture. The knowledge it provided about the subject is much needed now as the subject has become a new subject matter of the culture at the present time. The reason is that every aspect of evolution of the culture exposes new things about the subject that makes renewing understanding essential, because in most of the new endeavors of that culture depends on the subject. Western Culture is still a vibrant, active, and evolving culture; therefore, for psychoanalysis to maintain its renowned importance it has to reoccupy its empty place in that culture and resume contributing to its main objective: *defining the human subject.*

Between the nineteen thirties and the nineteen sixties, psychoanalysis was on the verge of radical changes. The changes came, particularly from being the center of a rich and active network of human sciences; exchanging insights, facts, new knowledge about the subject who discovered that he exists in a relationship with counterpart of his making. Psychoanalysis was the dynamo of the Western culture at that time. Being in linkage with equally inspired thinkers and scientists put the clinical aspect of the discipline in context and a perspective, and many discoveries about the intrapsychic, narcissism, and transference were extensively elaborated. The links psychoanalysis had with the rest of the human sciences were renewed and revealed that it is still as important to the culture as a whole, not only to its patients and their psychotherapy. Recently, with the disintegration of psychoanalysis into schools, psychoanalysts and the psychoanalytic organization reduced Freud to a historical moment, instead of realizing and recognizing Freud as a significant contributor to the Western culture and the most insightful thinker in it, regarding the subject's true self. Lately his psychology of the intrapsychic was deemed by psychoanalysts as 'passé' and the interpersonal theories were declared by many as more relevant psychoanalysis. Psychoanalysis became an epistemology that has a short history, which started and ended with Freud.

This view of psychoanalysis is dangerously faulty because Freud was not a moment in history; he was a stage in an ongoing cultural evolution. As we will see next in this chapter, Freud was a ring in the chain of thinkers who built this culture. His rightful position in the Western culture is that of a link with the philosophers and thinkers that came before him, a link that kept both psychoanalysis and philosophy active in defining the subject. I will frame this idea as a central question in my attempt at approaching the theory of the human subject as the theory of psychoanalysis. Is Freud a ring in a chain of interlinked thinkers and philosophers, or is he a lonely ring without any attachment that could decide his place or psychoanalysis's place in this culture?

My immediate answer right away is: *Freud is an important ring in a chain of great thinkers who led him to where he started contributing to his culture.* His ring was forced to link to other rings despite the analysts' denial that those other rings belonged to psychoanalysis. Freud's ring is open now for many other rings, which need to connect to his in a serious push toward a theory of the human subject, and to a novel future for psychoanalysis.

A Brief Account of the Western Philosophical Movement

I will deal here with an extremely modest account of a string of gradual and incremental evolution of modern Western philosophy. It is meant to make the analysts who are not interested in anything besides psychoanalysis have an idea, if not a background, of where Freud was starting from. This account shows that the human subject was already an issue of interest before psychoanalysis claims to have discovered it. Therefore, this brief account is not meant to inform or expose the philosophies of those philosophers, but to show psychoanalysts that their preoccupations with the subject was an uninterrupted linkage of efforts of great thinkers who built on each other's work. They formed the heritage that Freud was a late significant ring in it.

It is useful to keep in mind that the theory of the subject started and advanced before Freud, and that the most of what he did, and almost unintentionally, was uncovering a very central attribute of the subject that was awaiting discovery. He did not discover the unconscious because it was already discovered in France; he uncovered its complex and complicated nature. He also established the unconscious as the new principle of the discipline of psychoanalysis.

Western culture started from the notion that the human subject is alive but not fully or really extant (see chapter one). There was also a gradual awareness of the significance of consciousness in the subject. However, he was not emoted or individually identified or recognized. The human subject was there to examine his world and learn about it, to make changes to it and use it. He lived and created a human life that is distinct from animal life, but still had no sense of being or ownership of his personal consciousness of that material world. It took the western subject few centuries of progress to first ask: what about *me*, the subject himself? I know that I exist but what does it mean that I have an existence? Could *I* take myself and my existence as issues to examine?

Those questions were the beginning of the subject's evolution toward subjectivity, which till that time was absent in the social system. Tradition classified human subjects on the basis of their social position, and accordingly the subject acquired some additional qualifications to his simplistic sense of being, but not more awareness of self. He was human and Christian, but also a serf or a land owner. However, the issue of identity was opening on other attributes that needed defining. A modern reviewer of the history of the Western world would be amazed by how the previously unaccounted for passive citizen built the foundation of freedom and equality, that have become the core of the Western subject centuries later. The early citizen of this culture inched slowly but very detrimentally towards emancipation from servitude and building a culture of individuality, rights, and ultimately finding his subjective identity.

Around the twelfth century theology became a scene of many interests, in particular interpreting the religious texts and extracting from them hidden meanings and messages (hermeneutics) of the subject and his believes. Christian philosophy was the womb that gave birth to the idea, act, and technicalities of interpretation. This budding interest was in the subject's interest in his own unconscious explication of himself. He treated the religious texts as unconscious sense of being that constituted his consciousness then. Mastering the art of scholarly interpretations expanded to studying other issues in the same manner. The scholastic methodology led – in the fourteenth century – to the age of philosophy. Old and modern concerns of the human subject became issues of methodical investigation including the methods themselves. The thinkers of scholasticism realized that their plight is a collaborative and sustained effort that relies on each other, and no one effort could achieve the aspired answer to *what* and *who* is the subject. The previously non-excitant subject suddenly ignited the age of philosophy, and the questions mentioned above became the 'raison d'être' of philosophy.

In a surprising shift the subject took ownership of his consciousness. The scholastics extensive examination of the subject's mind and its manifestation was not enough for the philosophers' project. Consciousness and its content became an inherent issue in the subject's being. Nonetheless, the scholastic undertakings led to an old question: how could I be sure that my consciousness is not deceiving me and my reason is enough to confirm my subjectivity! This was a more sophisticated and elaborate form of the question asked three thousand years before by Thales Meletus (chapter one). As that question ignited Greek philosophy this new question about our *presence* ignited the age of philosophy in the sixteenth century.

The Cogito and the Subjects

René Descartes (1596–1650) reformulated the question with a slight twist: how I could be sure that my own being is true. The answer was deceptively simple: *I think, therefore I am;* a statement dubbed 'the Cartesian Cogito.' The doubt in one's existence affirms his existence: thinking of my existence is the proof that I am existing[1]? Since the Cogito, the subject who was always considered an ontological entity is now – and fundamentally – a duality of a thinker and a thinker of thinking, i.e., he does not only exist but can also prove his existence. The issue of certainty was no longer an issue of certainty about objects, but about the subject who has to discover certainty to ascertain himself as an object. Descartes was quite insightful when he decided that we have to

---

[1] A common misunderstanding of the Cogito comes from missing that Descartes was out to resolve the issue of the proof of certainty. Missing this point made some psychoanalysts distort Descartes's whole endeavour, thus they distorted their understanding the central conceptions in psychoanalysis. They (R. Stolorow, et al. 2001) alleged that Descartes "picture the mind as an objective entity that has an inside containing contents... a thinking thing." What seemed as Descartes isolated mind or the *I think* in the cogito was the nominal reference to the observing *I*. By acknowledging that the subject is a duality of I think and I am giving the inter-subjective analysts a straw to hang on the impossibility of separating the subject from his mind. The subject and his mind are engaged similarly and equally in the ongoing psychical life. Yet, one is the doing and its counterpart is noticing. It is also of importance to put Descartes in the framework of his time, where the linguistic subtitles were not the same as in our time. We can now avoid making mistakes of the type he is accused of doing.

be certain of our existence first to be able to be ascertaining whatever certainty we would seek and affirm after. The discovery of the subject started at that point when the subject became *conscious* of uncertainty and the necessity of dealing with it. I have to underline the similarity between this beginning of a theory of the subject and the beginning of analytic work itself, when the patient becomes aware of the uncertainty of his consciousness.

A chain of philosophers addressed the challenge that the Cogito posed, and dealt with the gap in the duality of the active *I* of the I am of thinking, and the observing *I* of the 'am.' At this point I suspect that psychoanalysts will be asking their main question: what has that to do with psychoanalysis? A temporary answer is: *Could we have had psychoanalysis in the first place without Descartes Cogito and the duality of the subject that is implicit in it?* Could the French school of the Salpêtrière have talked of splitting of consciousness without the Cogito being part of the French culture? Could Freud have discovered psychoanalysis without the notion of split consciousness? The answer to all that is no, the Cogito was the beginning of a philosophical journey that eventually got stuck till the coming of Freud.

A brief account of the efforts the thinkers and philosophers made in dealing with the duality of the human subject is a very valuable step-by-step guide to discovering the duality of the conscious-unconscious, which was Freud's 'lot in life.' Without recognizing duality, it would have been impossible for him to think about an existence of something pertaining to the human subject and resides outside his consciousness. He would not have just stumbled on in it accidentally, casually, or fortunately, because if he did, he would not have realized that he did. After Descartes's initial blow to the barrier between scholastic philosophy and the exploration of the subject, philosophers began a great trek toward the core of the subject's duality. I tried to select, from few philosophers I have chosen, some of their notions about that duality, which related to the psychoanalytic preoccupations, so I keep evident the link between philosophical thinking and Freud's work, and make the incremental advancement from philosophy to psychoanalysis reasonable.

The Forerunners of Psychoanalysis

Spinoza (1632–1677) founded his philosophy on a single and only substance that has the basis and the multiplicity of attributes that constitute the reality in which we live, i.e., nature or God (no cause-effect issues in that). His monotheism had one system to contend with that underlay the reality of everything. However, the subjects still had two attributes that deal with reality: through material and non-material realities. The subject in that sense is both mind and body[2] but in unison. Damasio (2003) put it slightly differently: "The reference to a single substance [in Spinoza] serves the purpose of claiming mind as inseparable from body. Both created, somehow, from the same cloth. The reference to two attributes, mind and body, acknowledged another duality: the distinction of two kinds of phenomena, a formulation that preserves an entirely sensible 'aspect' dualism, but rejects substance dualism" (p. 209). Spinoza had the notion that the mind contained the capacity to perceive facts but could also perceive its perception (apperception), or become conscious of its own capacity to generate consciousness. This was a more elaborate way of putting the Cogito, because duality was only a manifestation of a different mode of duality in the subject, and not in his objects or his material reality. Spinoza's thinking was affected by a Cartesian difficulty regarding the issue of causality, which resulted from separating the predicate of existence (I am) from its attributive (I think), thus a causative relation was unavoidably entertained and brought to focus.

Spinoza specified a third duality based on the previous two: a duality between cause and reason. Perception dealt with the world and led to the need of uncovering its causes, while apperception dealt with the reason of things (its grammar!). This third dualism engendered a fourth duality: even though brain and mind were inseparable, they were two distinct entities, physical and psychological. In spite of Spinoza's monotheistic understanding of reality, including the reality of the subject, he resorted to the notion of attributes to account for the multiplicity of the dualities of that subject. Spinoza, in spite of his basic premise, was sensitive to the impossibility of dealing with any subjective attribute without keeping in perspective its double or counterpart (dormant). Spinoza's subject engendered many questions for others to answer.

Leibniz (1646–1716) took a different way in dealing with the dualities encountered in any attempt at understanding the subject, as the Cogito highlighted. Instead of examining the subject's duality, he started by constituting a theory – a theoretical proposition – that if applied to the subject could provide an explanation of his dualities. The proposition was that the world comprised self-contained units of force, from which everything is formed. He called those units 'Monads.' Each Monad was a duality of perceptive and desiring states, and the subject is a constituent duality of all those dualities. In those dualities, perception was geared toward facts and was distinguished from apperception, or reasoning the perceived. The reason of the truth of a fact is referred to the principle of 'sufficient reason' (nothing happens without a reason). The principle of reason was a passive quality of the mind,

---

[2] See chapter nine for more on the duality of mind-body.

which makes it just a mirror reflecting the factual world around it. Truth of reason, on the other hand, refers to the principle of identity, which he stipulated to be a thing that could not also be its opposite. This principle was innate and an active attribute of the mind (apperception). Leibniz's conception of the dynamics of perception and apperception put the duality of the subject in a context of polarities that are qualitatively discontinuous but hierarchically connected (quantitatively). Monads were organized in a hierarchy in which the Monad of the soul, for instance, was above that of the body, and exerted control over it. His theory led to a concept of *unconsciousness* that was closer to the desiring aspect of the Monads (or Freud's *Instinct*), which does not abide by reason. The 'unconscious' in that definition could come back in other states of consciousness, like dreams, for instance. Leibniz's philosophy, though monotheistic in form, was dualistic in substance. He dabbled with the nature of the intrapsychic more than a hundred years before Freud.

Kant (1724–1804), as he himself stated, was the Copernicus of philosophy. He shifted the duality of the subject's world into a duality in the subject's mind. In other words, he did not accept that the world imposes on the subject a dual approach to perceiving it; rather, the subject's mind is only capable of a two-phase approach to reality. In his theory, the human subject was endowed with 'sensibility,' which is a ected by things as they are. Although the mind receives the quality of things passively, its sensibility generates intuitions, which is an active and antithetical quality of the mind. Intuition begets the understanding of what was sensibly perceived. Intuition in turn is a product of 'apriori' categories in the mind that reconfigure the sphere of objects into a sphere of concepts, thus engendering thought. Knowledge does not conform to the sphere of objects; rather, it is the objects that conform to sensibility and the categories innately utilized in forming categories, concepts, and thought. Sensibility and understanding are interpretation of the world, which makes our reason accept that we do not perceive 'things in themselves' but only things as they appeared to us (represented). Kant introduced the concept of imagination (which transcends perception) as the compromise between sensibility and understanding; it is an act of *interpretation*. Interpretation provides the synthetic categories of causality, reality, reciprocity, etc. It allows perception to become thought, thought to become understanding, and understanding to become judgment (Brentano and Freud's notion of the pleasure principle. Freud, 1920g).

Fichte (1762–1814) thought that Kant did not explain the link between sensation and understanding and did not expound on the derivatives of the innate categories that organize our knowledge. However, he took Kant's notion of '*I* think' as the start of any experience and embarked on a very novel metaphysical trip of the nature of duality. He stated that both the world and *I* are strangers to each other, though it is the *I* that has the ability to comprehend both the external (the non-*I*) and the mental states (the *I* itself). The *I* that comprehends the mental states does not do that transcendentally and not by taking the mental as an object of its action, because the *I* is not a thing or a substance. It is an activity of self-positing that exists in self-awareness but is continually in a dialectical engagement with the non-*I* (the antithesis), a dialectical negation to a rm the existence of each and both (Freud's ego as negation (1925h). A second duality is thus born: the *I* has to negate itself in order to become the synthesis of that duality. The most important outcome of the dialectics of the *I*, in Fichte's expansion of the issue of understanding, is the double notion of the *I* as a subject and as an object (me). He considered the *I*'s understanding to be geared toward causality because causality is an internal understanding, while reason is aimed at the external world (note his reversal of Spinoza's formulation). Reaching this stage of dealing with the subject needed a leap forward to put 'that' subject in a perspective after being just a phenomenon to be studied. The subject had to be understood.

Hegel's (1770–1831) approach to understanding the subject was more straightforward and insightful. He considered the entire history of man's intellectual development a continuous e ort of the mind to knowing itself. He perceived knowledge as a process that is dialectical and not just dynamic, as his predecessors conceive of it. At any stage of the mind's advancement toward unravelling knowledge, ignorance has to be removed by the force of that knowledge (the *process* in psychoanalysis!). Thus, a kind of new knowledge emerges as a synthesis of the previous knowledge and the ignorance it removed: a dialectical entanglement between a thesis and its anti. Nothingness becomes the antithesis of being and forces the mind to discover itself. This dialectical motion produces rationality, which is the equivalent of reality. Therefore, making anything real is intrinsically making it rational. Hegel's philosophy was a statement of making a philosophy of the subject a philosophy of self-creation (in that meaning psychoanalysis and psychotherapy are mutually contradictories!).

Fichte's and Hegel's dialectics were not sufficient to analyzing the subject's duality. There was no firm clue to what comes first: does the mind separate the thesis from the antithesis or do the two conflicting sides of reality create the dialectical mind? Which of the two elements of such duality represents and constituted the thesis, so we could constitute a clear polarity of thesis-antithesis that permits further analysis? Even if the notion of a link between the thesis and the antithesis could be considered a synthesis of sorts, this synthesis would not lead to anything of value. The link as a synthesis would be nothing more than an additional element of both the represented and the representation. However, in Fichte's philosophy the subject took center stage once again by being where the dialectics of its nature exits. The subject turned out to be the creator of the link and the one who should discover it. His success or even his failure in discovering that link meant, implicitly, an e ort to discovering his 'self.' The subject who was supposed to know has become the curious object of that knowledge, and the process thus was susceptible to getting to a gradual halt. *The subject had become both an object of knowledge and the subject who is supposed to attain that knowledge.* Both were waiting for someone to find a way to introduce them to each other and unlock that impasse.

Schelling (1775–1854 took the opposite position from Kant's view of where duality (ontologically) existed. He was of the opinion that duality is a quality inherent in nature because nature effectuates and expresses itself according to the law of 'polarities,' or as pairs of opposite, though complementary, forces. He talked about 'unconsciousness' in the context of a condition that strives toward its negation, i.e., becomes conscious. Thus, he posited it in the framework of a duality with consciousness (opposite to what Freud did when he put consciousness in a state of negating unconsciousness). He considered the whole nature of life a teleological advancement toward consciousness. Thus, the unconscious, in his consideration, was a manifested finality that is a process of teleological advancement toward consciousness. It is not clear whether he meant that nature has that quality of unconsciousness or he conceived of nature as the unconscious state of the human mind, which strives toward consciousness (see Hegel).

Schopenhauer (1788–1860 viewed the world as a representation of the way the principle of su cient reason (Leibniz) is applied in the four root areas of thinking: the physical world we perceive; judgment or the logical sphere where truth lies; spatial and temporal intuitions, and motivation and will. Understanding the laws of causality led him to understanding their conceptual representation (Vorstellogen), which was secondary to abstraction. Schopenhauer distinguished between the thing (the phenomenal) and the thing-in-itself (the nominal). He applied that duality to the subject and came up with the idea that the nature of the nominal subject is unconscious, and that *the unconscious is a storehouse of motivations and desires,* whereas the phenomenal subject was consciousness, even if only of part of himself. Thus, the 'unconscious' was reflective of the subject's truth and will. Schopenhauer's unconscious was very much antecedent of Freud's id (a reservoir of the instincts).

Von Hartmann (1842–1906 tried to find the common ground between Schopenhauer and Kant, so he eventually agreed with Schopenhauer that *the ultimate reality of the subject was unconscious*, but he did not agree that it was a 'blind' will. Von Hartmann viewed the unconscious as having two coordinated functions: will and idea. Will was unable to produce any teleological processes and was merely accountable for the sense of existence of the *that*, or the world. Idea was incapable of objectifying the world hence it accounted for the 'what' of the world or the nature of that world. He suggested that the end of 'telos' is the liberation of the idea from its servitude to the will, therefore, it becomes possible to advance toward consciousness. Will – to him – was more like the power of the aim of the *Trieb*, while idea is the object of that *Trieb*.

In the nineteenth century, German idealistic metaphysics started to show features of fatigue. Yet it reached the crucial point in the Western culture of striving for addressing the subject's perception of himself as an object of consciousness, and his consciousness of his consciousness. This point revealed an intrinsic and definitive gap – if not an abyss – in any of the dualities philosophers thought of focusing on. This gap demanded bridging after the enlightenment that was reached. Metaphysics in general, and in the issue of the subject's duality were going through unavoidable shifts and turns. Accepting the notion of the subject's duality directed the thinkers to the issue of the corollaries of the duality in other aspect of the culture. One of the most prominent consequences was putting the subject within the context of his society and its impact on everything he experiences. Karl Marx (1818–1883) – a materialistic Hegelian – did that and changed German philosophy from metaphysics to social physics. He looked at that gap in its historical-social context to show that societies have a group spirit that is parallel and also dialectical to the manner and spirit of the subject. Dialectical materialism and what he referred to as turning Hegel's dialectics downside up, reveals that societies have processes that create mass self-awareness. It has its own consciousness and blind spots, and is tempting to reach some understanding of its dynamics in almost the same way we do with the individual's consciousness[3]. Marx was critical of Hegel's notion that reality is a product of

---

[3] Analyst who try to deal with social phenomena make the mistake of using the Freudian models of conflict, motivation, defense mechanisms, relational structures, even the unconscious dynamics in treating and explaining socio-historical events. Socio-historical events create the individual and are not created by the individual. They could explain some psychical changes in generations of individuals but cannot be explained by those changes in individuals.

ideas, which makes thought processes independent acts of the spirit (mind). His penetrating insights into the limitations of Hegel's idealism (ideas as the active agents in a process) emphasized that the subject's consciousness and his being are determined by the material social conditions he lives. Marx's meant that the subject is a product of his society, not a pre-existing entity of the society. He was the first philosopher to indirectly (unconsciously) raised the issue of the intrapsychic, or the structure of the individual as product of his social milieu.

In Marxism, the subject is an entity that is molded by its history and society, thus whatever the subject is, his 'potentials' will be arranged according to the demands put on him from his society. The subject is thus the elaboration of the workings of the social forces. This conception is the underpinning of Freud's exploration of the role of the interfamilial dynamics in forming the subject's psychical life.

Bergson (1859–1941) extended the line of thinking of the duality a little further (but not much). He differentiated between experience that deals with static objects that exist in space and constitute the world of matter, and experience of nonmaterial objects, such as ideas, which are flexible and exist in a dimension of subjective time. In the former, the subject's experience tends to apply reason to understanding, while intuition is the subject's approach to the nonmaterial objects, such as ideas. Bergson's approach was of the twentieth century's perspective of the subject's duality. The phenomenologists and the existentialists (e.g., Husserl and Heidegger, 1889–1976) considered the subject a dilemma more than a duality. They saw the subject's being-in-the-world, or within his own context, as a key to comprehending his crisis. The essence of the dilemma was still a gap, which its very existence point to the link between the subject's consciousness of his unconsciousness and whatever was not yet in his consciousness. Foucault called it the *unthought* (1982). In other words, duality became a connotation of schism in the subject that gives him a bi-existence, which was to the existentialists the main issue in the ontology of the subject.

Structuralism was the answer to most of what the philosophers strove to integrate in a theory of the subject. It took the place of functional thinking and the effort to dealing with the Cartesian duality, and introduced the subject as a being that is a translation of an extraordinary text.

Conclusion

This very brief exposition of some thinkers' dealings with the subject shows where Freud, and psychoanalysis in general, will eventually link. The subject emerged from oblivion as a unique entity in his own right to become a phenomenon of consciousness that separates him from the rest of the animal kingdom, and from the material world. The philosophical work about the human phenomena gradually focused the light on the nature of subjectivity. The subject became the object of choice for philosophical speculations. Those thinkers, which did the speculating after Descartes, treated the subject as the owner of his consciousness, which was an issue of limitless possibilities. The great thing Western philosophers did was realizing that the human subject was the being who reflected his nature; reflected what he is and how he is. They observed, examined, speculated, and explained what they encountered in thinking about that human nature and its functioning within the subject. The formation of human nature came in the form of attributes of the subject and were gradually coming to a point of acquiring new names that signify their depth, new depth. Nevertheless, the philosophers were unable to go further. From what their work highlighted, we can see *now* that what was missing in reaching better and new formation of human nature was the unconscious component that is the unique qualification of the subject; the human subject.

As a creation of that culture, Freud realized that what he was doing in hypnosis and in listening to his patients has that missing elements, which the philosophers were missing. Just before we get any further, we have to acknowledge that without the heritage that created the subject of the Western culture and the unfulfilled philosophical project to understand his formation, it would have been impossible for Freud to notice the unconscious in the subject, in its psychoanalytic meaning. Therefore, both Freud and the subject matter of his work are cut of the same cloth that philosophical heritage is made of.

Every philosopher in the list of the founders of the Western heritage uncovered an aspect of what is human in the human subject. They reached the point where duality had to be 'meaningful,' i.e., to find its explanation not only in philosophy but outside its sphere too. The gap within the dualities of the subject – starting with the nineteen century – was no longer merely a philosophical concern but proved to be an element in the happiness and unhappiness of the subject and the society. Another way of putting it, thinkers became more inclined to think of the human tragedy as a manifestation of gaps in the subject's *living* experience. They needed to find what could bridge them. The birth of the notion that psychological problems are health issue (Pinel), somehow removed the subject from the sphere of philosophy and put him in the realm of medicine and human sciences.

The work of the French school of medicine in the late years of the nineteenth century introduced two very significant and novel ideas about the subject. The gaps in his dualities are manifestation of splitting of consciousness (which was a very new and different conception of that function) and that that split conscious points to the existence of a dormant isolated part of the subject that is not talked about, because no one was able to understand its language. Therefore, the subject's dualities had a better chance to be comprehended if we could find that dormant part (hypnotism was the first attempt at searching for it). The subject's duality was getting nearer to getting a meaning. It became obvious that the human subject is also his own counterpart that is residing next to his awareness of his being. The problem was to get the counterpart to communicate with his subject to complement each other.

Freud discovered the meaning of the two novelties: splitting of consciousness indicates the existence of two systems of mental functioning: consciousness and unconsciousness, and the dormant part of the subject is an unconscious counterpart of the active conscious subject. The duality of the subject was no longer the issue; the gap within the duo in that duality and the communication between the two constituents, the lack of that communication, became the true issue in the culture of the subject.

It is obvious from the brief account of the philosophical journey from Descartes to Freud's that Western culture was waiting for that thinker who will make such communication happen. Freud was there and managed to make the counterpart speak to us and tell us what he is and what we are. Psychoanalysis was born only then. It still remains up to psychoanalysts to accept that psychoanalysis is not an isolated intellectual event and realize that its survival depends not on limiting its theoretical filed to its practice, or limiting its theory to psychopathology. This change would show that limiting its learning to the tradition of the institutes of psychoanalysis and some academic programs that teach psychotherapy is sentencing it to death. *Psychoanalysis is a theory of the human subject* and is connected to several other fields of the humanities, and their healthy interlinks essential to their own future.

Chapter Four
The Subject's Basic Duality and Narcissism
I and Me

Taking psychoanalysis back to its roots in philosophy is usually received unenthusiastically by clinical psychoanalysts. Nonetheless, there are a number of undeniable facts that could not be ignored in that regard. Philosophy's stipulation of the subject's duality is not a hypothesis or a proposition; it is a find. The subject duality was acknowledged even before organized religions' concepts of good and evil and right and wrong. Religion did not discover the new duality of the subject; it gave it names like body and soul. However, the philosophers' explanation of the subject's attributes made duality a *find*, because it was there unnoticed in the way they noticed it. Duality was inherent in the human mind and the subject could not have dealt with the manifest content and its latent meaning if he was not ready to approach his world this way. When the subject approached himself as an object – in the age of philosophy – he faced duality in another context. It is a duality that has a gap between the subject and himself because he is also an object. '*I am (me) thinking.*' This find of what was always there caught the attention of the thinkers in the age of philosophy and made them note the dualities within the subject's identity.

They also noted that the subject has a proclivity and a compulsion to turn a percept into a concept. This tendency is the basis of the birth of language and its complement, interpretation. We are able to see from the history of dealing with the object – as one of the entities in our world – that bridging the gap between the manifest of the object and its latent is basically missing. The process that moves the subject from the object to its meaning is his own act and responsibility. After a brief account from Descartes to Husserl, we can see that Freud came to explain that process by inserting in it what was lacking till then: the unconscious. The link between the two sides of the gaps, in the life of the subject, is formed from conscious efforts and unconscious mechanisms.

Psychoanalysis, thus, substantiates its natural extension to the philosophical endeavor.

A third find is that philosophy is not the opposite of anything in particular to rationalize the psychoanalysts' reluctance to belong to it, or admit that psychoanalysis relates to philosophy. Philosophy is the seat of all knowledge. Philosophers were – in the age of the enlightenment – the physicists, the chemists, the apothecarists, and the thinkers of most of the other fields of knowledge. Philosophical knowledge evolved to become professions and then sciences. We should not forget that methodology, the fabric of physical sciences, was once the work of some scholarly thinkers of the past. Physical sciences are not considered part of philosophy anymore because they deal with the subject as an object of nature and mange to come up with 'functional' theories about his life-manifestations. The prevailing narrow understanding of philosophy as the non-scientific aspect of human knowledge made analysts try to distance themselves from it. Analysts cannot do that without affecting psychoanalysis negatively. They leave psychoanalysis in a lurch: it is neither a physical science nor a branch of any organized knowledge. However, if psychoanalysts insist on detaching themselves from philosophy, they should consider psychoanalysis a human science. This would not become a straightforward act: the subject's attributes have to be 'objectified' first for other nomothetic sciences to study it in the traditional experimental model.

The way psychoanalysts are trained in IPA institutes does not qualify them to turn their training into an independent profession of psychotherapy. Studying the subject, which is the subject matter of psychoanalysis, is not part of their formation. Whatever is related to that topic is not extensive enough to produce a good theory of dynamic psychopathology. It is also not geared to make the analyst come up with issues that science could submit to the rigorous methodology of research. Therefore, the analytic organization(s) should be serious about the crisis of psychoanalysis and the possibility of its deterioration. They should give a serious look at the roots of their discipline in philosophy to form a good idea of training in institutes.

The Place of Psychoanalysis in Epistemology

The claim that psychoanalysis belongs to the field of mental health is historically justifiable, but is unjustified by in anything else in the field of mental health.

The beginning of psychoanalysis came as response to the French early theory of psychiatry which was based on the splitting of consciousness[1]. Charcot's work with hypnosis, Janet's interpretation of hysteria, and the school of hypnosis in Nancy were all done in the field of medicine. Freud continuation of that movement in Vienna was also more medical than non-medical. However, none of the discoveries in that movement – in all that time – was of any medical nature or value. It is not enough to call psychoanalysis a medical discipline just because the first ones who worked on its subject matter were physicians. In hindsight, discovering the splitting of consciousness had to come first from examining patients (the ones with split consciousness) and physicians were the only ones who were permitted to see patients. So, it was natural that psychoanalysis becomes associated with medicine. However, the discoveries that emanated from hypnosis in the late nineteen hundred did not relate to medicine, but did not dovetail with the philosophical dualities either. Nevertheless, the subject's duality, which is the philosophy's contribution to the theory of the subject, did not acquire any credible importance until psychoanalysis underlined its pervasiveness in the psychological life of the subject: healthy or sick.

Most clinical psychoanalysts accepted the general notion of the subject's duality because it was useful in supporting the duality of the conscious-unconscious. Duality within consciousness was only one of the features of the human subject and was not the foundation of the rest of his constituents. Psychoanalysts did not realize, or maybe just ignored, that the duality of conscious-unconscious is product of more basic and elementary dualities in the human subject. In other terms, duality as the key find of the subject in philosophy was taken up by the psychoanalysts as a casual occurrence, not as a basic condition. They frame it in their functional thinking when it was actually introducing the structural vision of the subject. However, it was not feasible for the culture of the subject to pass lightly over the find of the duality of the subject, as it was not possible for psychoanalysts to just consider duality a useful approach to the study of the subject. Western culture entered the stage of philosophy already looking for the complement of the scholastic phase and evolved to reach the stage of psychoanalysis, which in a proper conception is a structural theory of the subject. Psychoanalysis is an evolution of several aspects of unconsciousness that was waiting for further advancemen[2].

---

[1] Psychiatry in Germany was based on the distinction between thought and effect and the pathological conditions in that duo.

[2] The crisis of psychoanalysis is fundamentally a product of a problem closely linked to the refusal to put in consideration the roots of psychoanalysis in

The theory of the subject is predicated on the issue of duality, berceuse before establishing the subject's duality he was just an ontological entity (a man, a sinner, an astronomer, etc.), like all other entities in existence (mammals, primate, etc.). However, the subject's eventual awareness of his existence resulted in an awareness of consciousness. Consciousness is the subject's state of separateness from all other creatures. Consciousness and the subject's ownership of his consciousness created a new curiosity about him. Freud, shortly after abandoning hypnotism, was able to discern the patient's dualities in their regular speech, their dreams, their slips of the tongue, even in the subjects' jokes, etc. Psychoanalysis integrated philosophical dualities in their own view of the subject. This shift happened in very subtle and unnoticed way (almost unconsciously). It became evident that there was more to the subject than what he reveals of himself even to his own observing *I*. The link between the subject and 'that' complement in his duality became essential in any understanding of the subject. Freud noticed this fact and understood it partially by saying: "in the individual's mental life someone else is invariably involved, as a model, as an object, as a helper, as an opponent, and so from the very first individual psychology in this extended but entirely justifiable sense of the word is at the same time social psychology as well" (Freud, 1914c, p.70). Any complete understanding of the subject had to contend with two entities; the other within the subject's duality and the other that has always been external and the only known other to others.

The philosophical endeavors of defining the subject showed that every time a duality was identified an implicit duality within it shows the direction to continuing the search. Spinoza's subject was a duality of thought and extension, and Kant's intuitiveness was a duality of apriori and posteriori. The most significant imbedded duality in the duo of the subject's existence was what Fichte's differentiated between *I* and the non-*I* or the world, which introduced the distinction between the *I* that comprehend the world and another *I* that is supposed to comprehend both the world and that *I* which exists in the world. In simple psychoanalytic terminology, the conscious *I* engenders or is accompanied by another *I* that enables the differentiation between *I* think (feel, etc.) and *I* am thinking (feeling, etc.); a conscious *I* to conscious consciousness. It got clearer that every *I* has a counterpart that is also an *I* but acts as if it is another. The desiring *I* has a counterpart that regulates the relationship between

---

philosophy. What is taught in the training institutes is limited – to a great extent – to psychoanalysis as a profession. The profession of psychoanalysis is only an aspect of it. Psychoanalysis is the doge that is waged by its tail; training.

the subject and his desiring *I*. Hence, the subject has to face 'three' fundamentals before starting to show the strains and tensions within himself.

The *first* duality is the duality of *I* not *I* (the world in Fichte) which exposes a gap of a certain characteristic. The subject always deals with a mental representation of the object (Kant) and learns about the object through that representation. The representation of the subject that would become his objective self is an interpretation that he has to deal with believing that it is the real *he*. In psychoanalysis, we examine those representations to discover how they were constructed and we look for the personal need that contributed to their constructions. Better, because representations are interpretations of the objects, they are disposed to being wrong or distorted. We should thus ask: what is the representation of the counterpart of the *I* since it is to the subject another? Our counterpart is to us another (the Lacanian unconscious), so it is still conceivable that it could be distorted representation of ourselves (in some cases this relationship is what Freud described to be between the ego and super ago). It is easier to advance the meaning if a theory by saying that the subject is an interpretation of ourselves which come across as our counterpart. The counterpart provides the link between the manifest *I* and the latent *I*, which is dormant within the duo of the subject.

The *second* duality is implicit in the first. In understanding the world, the subject sees it as objects. However, the objects – in the subject's experience – are representations. The subject establishes the link between the objects and their representations. Showers, represent to one watering the crop, and to another a nuisance. The links between the object and the representations are basic dualities of the life of the subject. However, once the subject worked up the world around him, those dualities change drastically: they become duality of antitheses. *The subject is the antithesis of the object or the world, thus the link between them becomes complex, dynamic, and most of all dialectally emergent.* The gap in the duality of watering the crop or the nuisance is direct displacements. This same duality, when worked up by the subject, creates several possible gaps, which bridging them proves to be a complex set of links related to a number of issues dependent on the meaning of the crop or the reason for the nuisance. Strait replacement could become the source of several more complex dualities that supersede a simple displacement. Representation signifies the object but the signifier itself gets into other sets of subjective links that include sets of signifiers. This notion reminds of free associating about a dream or an event, and the links that are established by the primary process.

The *third* duality is of an active *I* and its reflective counterpart. The *I* of the Cogito puts us face to face with the subject as the object in the subject matter of a theory. The *I* of thinking has to be recognized as *me* (who is thinking), which is the precondition for my existence. In other words, the subject's duality is a duality of the subject *I* and his dual entity as the object *me*. Bridging the gap between them depends on how the two could communicate. They both have the potential to communicate, but they have to understand each other to constitute one and the same human subject, a subject who knows his knowing self. This is the most significant and complex aspect of the theory psychoanalysis as a theory of the subject.

It is easy for psychoanalysts to envisage the multitudes of distortions that could happen in actualizing those three different dualities and relate that to what could happen in the unconscious links within each and between them.

I, Me, and the Other

Laplanche (1997) said, "Western philosophy, which can be encompassed by the general term 'philosophy of the subject,' has always stumbled over the problem of the other. For it, the otherness of the external world has always appeared doubtful, problematic, having to be deduced solely from the evidence of subjectivity… Western culture and its philosophy is the culture of the 'subject,' though its apparent interest has been in the subject as an object. The other in it is an object for the subject. However, the subject is another to himself too" (p. 653).

I pointed out before that in the earliest phases in the emergence of the human subject in Western culture the subject was a collective identity, determined by the collective status which the subject 'found himself' part of. The different and gradual studies of the subject showed that he got emancipated from his collective identity and 'individuated' in stages. There was *no existing other* before that happened because the *I* did not *feel* like an independent existence. When the subject existed as free entity the *I* created the *he* and the *they* as complemented modes of his existence. This was the preliminary duality of *I* and *the world*. But, in a surprising moment of human intuition, Descartes highlighted a duality within the *I* and the *I* that does the thinking about thinking. Unconsciously, the human subject separated those two constituents of his identity, which were before just modes of speaking. Quietly, the subject denoted to himself by two inseparable pronouns: *I* referred to his subjectivity, and *me* referred to his objectivity[3]. It just became obvious

---

[3] In Arabic 'ana' is the pronoun of the first person singular. The equivalent of me comes implicitly in the verb. However, there is another format for 'ana' which carries a firm distinction from the implicit pronoun which is 'Eyyay' (me myself).

that – unconsciously – the reflective *I* talks about *me* as another with all the distortions and defects we could encounter in talking about someone else. The problem of the other, or the other as problem, is a product of the Western culture's sudden awareness of the *subjectivity* of the subject. Analytically speaking we can notice the difference between *the subject talking to us* and *talking about himself to us*. Unnoticeably, social organizations rules and laws, literature and the other matters that pertained to the subject, widened the gap between *I* and *me* in the subject. The *me* gained the status of a counterpart, yet the relationship between *I* and *me* remained a puzzle.

The *I* denotes *me*, but the *me* connotes itself with all the subject's potentials and possibilities. There is a very important difference in this regard: the *I* tells about itself directly, but the *me* can only refer to itself. We are able to know our *I* directly but we do not know or know how to know *me* without something that reflects it to the *I*. The reflecting *me* functions mostly according to the primary process rules and does not function under the commands of the *I* with its secondary process rules. It reflects *something* unconscious in most cases and most parts, because the reference to the *I* is not limited to its active nature. The reflective indicator of the *me* is a reminder of Narcissus's reflection on the surface of the pond. What supports making that distinction between the two pronouns is the nature of the deception each could performs. Self-deception is universally done unconsciously, not consciously or deliberately. The *me* does not deliberately chose to hide its intentions or declare them, but likely it reveals more of itself if not stopped by the *I*. The two processes coexist in the subject and do not annul each other for the simple reason that they do not use the same psychical process of speech (expression). *I* could express anger verbally or physically and might hide that emotion for conscious reasons, but *me* would express it through a rise in blood pressure and a stammer. The gap between the *I* and the other has to be bridged by language, not necessarily verbal. The gap between *I* and *me* as a counterpart does not demand bridging. Thus, understanding the other takes place within the talking of the other (the patient does not know that he knows).

A theory of the subject has to have an explanation for this duality, because the subject is always aware of not knowing all of himself, and normally would like to know the rest of him (shown sometimes in seeking psychoanalytic therapy). Analytically speaking the 'patient' wants the *I* to know the *me,* so he could control its power of creating the neuroses. Because that endeavor is never fully reached the gap remains but in different degrees of alienation. The

---

This is the classical way of affirming that the doer is Anna. The distinction of the I and the me is mostly decided grammatically.

separation and estrangement of the *I* and *me* is the basis of the subject's neuroses and psychoses. Therefore, a theory of the subject should explain the subject in both sickness and health. We are the only creature who could become psychotic or neurotic, i.e., loses his mind and renders it incapable of knowing the rest of himself. Thinking of thinking, consciousness of consciousness, and awareness of one's existence suggest, even demands, examining the communication between the *I* and the *me*.

Communication with others uses shared linguistic means, verbal and non-verbal. Understanding, misunderstanding, failure to communicate with the other is not due the absence of a system of communication. It is due to distorted usage of the common communication system. We misunderstand each other not because the system of communication is deficient, but because the duality of the *I-me* in one of the two parties or both is messed up and does not allow clear undistorted communication. In those cases of miscommunication, the subject encounters first a basic miscommunication within himself; between his *I* and his *me* that supersedes any and all other communications. All the efforts to use introspection to discover *me* fails to get beyond realizing that the other within the duality of the subject is not like the other outside that entity. Therefore, self-analysis is a mirage until the speaker listens to himself, which in the best conditions is limited by the *I's* ability to separate from its counterpart.

The counterpart was always a problem in the field of psychopathology, before Freud. Firstly, the subject could not be reached by introspection because the counterpart spoke a different language, i.e., the language of the unconscious. The solution to this problem came about in an unexpected manner. After Pinel (1740–1826) broke the chains of the patients in the Salpêtrière hospital and refused to consider them victims of evil spirits or something external to their conditions, they, for the first time, became patients who suffer from diseases, i.e., the causes of their diseases should be found within their diseases. Thus, they were included in the traditional medical lexicon. It took a very short time for the enlightened psychiatrists in France to discover the way to use hypnotism to show that consciousness could split and create mental disorders (Hysteria in particular). One part of that split could disappear and reappear under hypnosis. So, they unintentionally and almost by accident discovered the unconscious. They were able then – through hypnosis – to remove aside the *I* to see what it is there behind. The subject was an entity that unconsciously has a counterpart. *The counterpart was the unconscious of the concerned patient.* Splitting of consciousness and considering one part of it as the other was a beginning of discovering that the dualities of the subject, which the philosophers exposed before, were not merely a philosophical issue but were more entrenched in any effort to explore and understand the 'subject,' healthy or sick.

The Counterpart and the Particularity of the Psychoanalytic Theory

Freud's paper on *Narcissism* (1914c) intrudes the idea of a primary phase of narcissism as the earliest stage in the subject's sense of existence. Primary narcissism is a state that is without lurking duality(ies); the newly born could vaguely pay attention to the world around him to activate that first duality. Instinctively, Freud brought to attention the assumption that the subject (the infant) and the object (the mother) are at the beginning one undifferentiated existence. For the infant to have any sense being – at that stage – it would not be separate from his sense of his mother's being. The caregiver, with his response to the infant needs and demands, identifies the infant to himself in a gradual way (you are good, you do not feel well, etc.). In primary narcissism, when the infant is still without an identity, the object or the other is a *double* or an object that is also of a narcissistic nature. Narcissism is the name Freud gave to the relationship between the infant and the caregiver: they are actually the double of each other as Narcissus and his reflection on the water were. Freud called the interest or libidinal investment in the double 'narcissism.'

Freud's introduction of the libido theory to his new understanding of narcissism swayed him away from its structuring power (a different issue that does not belong here). However, he maintained his view that narcissism is an issue that pertains to the emergence a sense of self and the double, i.e., narcissism is an issue of identifying the *I* and its doubles. In the paper of the *Uncanny* (1919h), he says: "the 'double' does not necessarily disappear with the passing of primary narcissism, for it can receive fresh meaning from the later stages of ego development" (235). The double that Freud talks about in the context of narcissism is the double of the subject. More precisely, *in narcissism the other is not a participant in a duality; the other is what the infant sees with fascination and forms from that fascination the notion that he (the infant) is another.* That double of the conscious *I* is experienced or sensed unconsciously by the infant, because there is nothing to him that would compare with. Even in adulthood, the primitive sense of being as a double could come back within the conscious sphere in a *parapraxis*. A slip of the tongue does not feel like being coming from the subject, but it feels as if it is the making of the counterpart or the double. The double is usually experienced as a stranger or someone other than the self, which produces a sense of

66

uncanniness. It is the unconscious *me*. Lacan identifies that cunningly by saying that *the unconscious is the other* (1977).

Although *I* and *me* together constitute the subject – in terms of the narcissistic state – they do not complement each other. They are in an antithetical relationship. If the *I* is conscious (I know what *I* wants, thinks, intends to do, etc.), the *me* is unconscious but knows what the *I* does *not* want to reveal or think. Freud, in a surprising intuition, not supported by any previous or known argument, expressed the relationship between *I* and *me* as the *I* is 'negation' or the negation of the *me* (Freud, 1925h). Better, Freud and consequently psychoanalysis in general came up with a very unusual observation about the subject. Any duality of the subject is a duality of conflict, of dialectic tension, of issues involved in ongoing processes. The psychoanalytic conception of the subject is an existence that is constantly thriving to reach stability, but is neither equipped to reach it nor tolerates its constancy. This view of the subject explains that the subject is not an ontological entity but an endless endeavor to reaching a conclusion that is not even achievable.

Recognizing the antithetical link between the subject and its double makes psychoanalysis the natural and logical extension of the philosophical revelation of the subject's duality. I have cited several dualities that emanate from the Cartesian Cogito and were revealed by different philosophers. In all those dualities, the link between the duo elements was antithetical creating a dynamic interaction of their thesis and antithesis. It is also noted that when both comprising theses where conscious, the link between them always remains unconscious. On the other hand, when one of the composing theses is unconscious, the link between them stays conscious but fails to reveal the purpose of the link. For instance, a person could get angry with his friend for certain behavior but the link between the anger and the friend's behavior could still remain unexplainable; usually anger does not reveal all that is there to make the person angry. The reason of the anger, in cases like that, is usually more than what the subject sees or explains. The conscious anger at a friend is unexplainable because something unconscious about the relationship stays unconscious. Whatever the subject calls a final reaction or causes of a reaction still shows that the link between the reason for the anger and the anger itself still contains an unarticulated unconscious component. The unconscious links between causes and effects – in structural theories – is not only pre-formed, it could also be post-formed (created as aftereffect).

The *counterpart* is a better term to use to explain, operationally, the dualities of the subject regardless of what the duality is about. The term counterpart has the implicit connotation of equivalence and the double, regardless of the function or the structure of the duality we talk about, Freud's thinking has been dialectical in method and style, and his vision of the intrapsychic dynamics of the subject was also dialectical in nature. Building his various theoretical models was also based on interaction between conceptions that allow – if not demand – developing and evolving. His whole text is variations on the theme of the dualities, giving a distinct impression that at any stage in the evolution of psychoanalysis it was – and still is – a project in progress. Ricoeur (1970) said, "A reader familiar with Hegelianism [the philosophy of dialects] cannot but help noticing the constant use of opposition in the structure of Freud's concepts [which are consistently dichotomous]. It is true that dichotomy is not necessarily a dialectic, and that in each instance the dichotomy has a different sense. But his [Freud's] style of opposition is intimately involved in the birth of meaning; the dichotomy is already dialectical" (p. 475).

The new polarity of the subject and the counterpart revealed a dialectical relationship between the subject's subjectivity represented in his reflective *I*, and his spontaneous tendency to transcend his subjectivity and undo it by turning the *me* into an object. Clinically speaking, a patient starts talking, stating his condition, but gradually changes to talk about *his* self. The analyst's sensitivity will make the distinction between listening to the patient's *I* and listening to the *I* talking about the *me*. We aspire in psychoanalyzing a patient to make the patient listen to himself talking about his counterpart, i.e., to make the conscious listen to its unconscious. The issue of the counterpart changed psychoanalysis from a philosophical problem to a problem that could and maybe should be sorted out first within a polarity of physical sciences versus human sciences. Capturing the subject in his positivistic states or merely as an ontological entity was a dream of the scientists[4]. Psychology, before the beginning of psychoanalysis, was promising some significant discoveries about the subject as a positivist entity through working on his behavior, cognition, emotions, etc., which were providing some facts about those aspects. That promising hope decimated when psychoanalysis underlined the intrusion of the unconscious (the counterpart) in the phenomena that were the topics of psychology.

Studying the subject as an object remained an unachievable undertaking because of his duality. Facilitating to the subject, transcending his being to

---

[4] Psychoanalysis has not yet moved from the clinical model to the science model. The science model would open psychoanalysis to the oriented, systematic, and expanded fields of studying the subject, instead of going in circles about what has already been learned about psychopathology.

being aware of being, and studying that transcendence became a psychoanalytic and an ethnological preoccupation. Thus, the subject has to be considered an issue in the humanities, which is separate from the main body of the physical sciences. Foucault (1970 made a perceptive remark about that polarity when he said, "In relation to the 'subject of sciences,' psychoanalysis and ethnology are rather 'counter-sciences'; which does not mean that they are less 'rational' or 'objective' than the others, but that they flow in the opposite direction, that they lead them back to their epistemological basis, and they ceaselessly 'unmake' that very subject who is creating and re-creating his positivity in the human science" (p. 379).

It is important to bring to attention something that psychoanalysis is experiencing for some time now due to the analysts' disregard of the specific nature of the unconscious (see chapter seven). Psychoanalysts are treating the unconscious (the counterpart or the other) the same way they treat consciousness; i.e. as positivistic entity or a specific psychical thing. They also do not consider the primary process a linguistic system of its own, and the language that is used by the counterpart. They look at it as a primitive formation or deviations from the usage of the secondary process. Psychoanalyst seems to be ignoring that the primary process, which is the constituent of the unconscious, is not a casual event in psychical life; it is the counterpart of regular speech, and exists in its very texture of any speech. The reason is that psychoanalysis is easier to understand if we continue to think of the unconscious as repressed material, as most analysts still do (see Fayek, 2013). The unintentional but relentless disregard of the idea that the counterpart is *not* repressed consciousness keeps psychoanalysts formulating psychical phenomena as dualities of similar conflicting psychical entities, and remains captive of functionality. The counterpart, as the duo of the person, reminds us of psychoanalysis as analysis of a dialectical link between an objective and subjective entities. The subject's duality is the function that generates his state of being.

Another feature in Freud's thinking is the place he gave to the process of mental representation, whatever the material he was dealing with. The notion that representation creates ideas (see Fichte's and Schopenhauer's representations of the unconscious) has become very important in Freud's classical theory of psychoanalysis (thing presentation and word presentation). In addition to the notion of representation, the concept of *Ich* or *I* was considered the subjective pronoun denoting the speaker, and the antithesis of the *me* or the objective subject or the person. Western culture was waiting for an intuition that could clear up that confusion and make the *I* and its counterpart differentiate without having to be separated. Thus, the subject could be properly defined. The idea of making the counterpart speak as *the objective duo of the subjective I*, or even as the other, was not a conscious aspiration of Freud, but there are indications that he assimilated that aspiration almost unconsciously; which we can find in the structural model of the tripartite theory of the subject (the ego, the id and the super ego).

Dialectics and mental representation were two concepts behind and about the duo *I/Me,* and the trio of the structural model of ego psychology. Freud was not intentionally looking for what constituted the impasse that the philosophers reached, yet he was inclined to look for representations of the subject and his counterpart. His four recognizable theoretical formulations (the cathartic theory, the *Trieb* and libido theory, the metapsychology theory, and finally the structural theory) were theories of representations of the subject. To make that feature in Freud's thinking clear, we can say that Freud was looking at the psychical phenomena as syntheses of conflicting wishes, where each wish is expressed as a representation, and stood as the antithesis of the other's wish. In the Dora case (Freud, 1905d), her two dreams – as he explained them – were the syntheses of conflicting wishes oscillating between temptation and anger, which was demonstrated practically in the premature termination of her analysis.

Einstein once said, "All great achievements of science must start from intuitive knowledge, namely, in axioms, from which deductions are then made... Intuition is the necessary condition for discovery of such axioms" (cited in Calaprice, 2000, p. 287). Freud knew where *not* to look, and what not to look for. However, he got the right intuitions to what to look for in whatever was in front of him and got the proper insights.

The Counterpart and the Intrapsychic

Freud's insight about the dream and its formation has something that is seldom if ever noticed. He stipulated that the dream fulfills two wishes; one from the day before the dream and a childhood wish that seems to support the previous one. This way, the dream should be considered the work of the subject who is conscious of his manifest wish (the day residue) and the childhood counterpart to that wish: *I* of now and *me* of before. When he endeavored to interpret one of his dreams made the subject (him) talk freely about the parts of the dream (divided into statement). The result was the work of the counterpart in the interpretation. The intuition was surprising because as he said years after getting it: "Insight such as this fall to one's lot but once in a lifetime" (Freud, 1900a – introduction to third edition, p. XXVII). The interpretation of the *Irma* dream revealed that a conscious wish has been fulfilled but only because it linked with a similar wish from childhood. In addition, the dream revealed some psychical workings that were performed surreptitiously and were what gave the dream both its visual content and verbal connotation. He called that work *dream-work* and revealed that the whole production used the 'primary processes' as its language. He had the insight that a dream fulfils a conscious wish of the subject and a wish of the counterpart, which is unconscious and existed before anything that has stimulated the dream to form.

When dream interpretation was proven to be possible and was revealed to the public, they were surprised because they realized, in an unexpected and strange way, that they (the subjects) have an active psychical life that is always awake and working in sleep. Dreams, maybe like everything else, are not merely psychical events but manifestations of something churning within all the subjects. *The Interpretation of Dreams* (Freud, 1900a) was the first and most convincing work that proved that the subject has an intrapsychic core. Paying attention to this point led to another major possibility. The intrapsychic combines the present and the past making the subject a scene of a dynamically active duality. The fact that we are what our intrapsychic life is and intrapsychic life could be reached through acts like interpreting dreams. Showing in an explicit way that the subject is amenable to being explored – instead of just speculated about – was the starting point in the life of psychoanalysis. Psychoanalysis became the method of revealing the intrapsychic life of the subject and the theory of what it reveals. Dream interpretation was the birth certificate of the concept of the intrapsychic life and the practical proof of the existence of the counterpart. The way Freud extrapolated from dreams the existence of a general intrapsychic life deserves special attention.

Revealing the existence of the intrapsychic is significant in its own right, but it also opened the minds to the fact that our whole life does not exist as some isolated psychological events, like dreams or symptoms. Freud's insight allowed him to make the counterpart speaks to the waking subject and confirm that it does the same in all the rest of the conditions of our psychological life. He showed that the subject always exists with his counterpart and they are linked with each other all the time. The flexibility of the primary process disguises the presence of the unconscious, but the unconscious could still be deciphered and be understood. In the *Irma* dream, all the physicians in the room made silly mistakes, which 'meant' that Freud is not the one who makes diagnostic mistakes. But the childhood megalomaniac counterpart is behind the metaphor of 'all of those physicians and also the patient' and not me is to be blamed. What needs to be underlined regarding Freud's intuition about dreams is that it related directly to the dualities of the subject and made the counterpart talk, define itself, and still maintain its dual property as the unconscious *me*. This inference adds to the needed discussion of the important point that the permeation of the intrapsychic in our existence is what makes the subject an issue of interpretation rather than explanation.

What is curious and intriguing about that discovery is that it did not come from Freud's work as a physician and psychotherapist. It came from unusual interest that was unrelated to his work as physician. Freud was impressed by the phenomenon of splitting of consciousness but for a short time. However, he did not see in all of that anything that could lead to understanding what makes the subject suffer from splitting of consciousness. He discovered in dream interpretation, parapraxes, and jokes a second and quite a di erent manner of expressing ideas (language) which the counterpart – the *me* of the *I* – uses to speak to the subject. In his contributions in the *Studies on Hysteria* (1895b), compared with Breuer's cases, he was attentive and sensitive to the patient's whole story more than in the direct links between the retrieved memories and the symptoms. *He was also able to read more in the symptoms than what was manifestly expressed* (The case of Fräulein Elisabeth von R.). He concluded from that case that the patient had done nothing more or less than looked for a symbolic expression of her painful thoughts and found that in the intensification of her su erings (1895 b, p. 152). He even presented the whole case of Katherina (ibid) – in which he did not use hypnosis – by reconstructing the patient's symptoms as the outcome of a sexual trauma and relied completely on two brief encounters with her. He mentioned in his presentation of the case history that "[it] is not so much an analyzed case of hysteria as a case solved by *guessing*" (1895 b, p. 133; italics added).

This step led Freud to make a very important distinction between the manifest (*I*) and the latent (*Me*). He did not pay attention to the significance of discerning the manifest-latent duality until he got the intuition that the *psychoneurosis is what creates the splitting of consciousness and not that splitting of consciousness is what causes the neurosis.* This was moving toward the structuralist side of theorizing. In other words, what had been considered the cause of the psychoneuroses was found to be its e ect; or it is 'me' that causes the sickness of the 'I.' Freud was not in any way prepared, trained, or advised to think about what was to come after the hypnosis stage. But it should be emphasized that the medical preoccupation with the limitations of the transcendence of consciousness, the way consciousness could become sick, its failure to keep the unconscious under control, and the derangement of the mind, led to taking a di erent path than the philosophers' path. Psychoanalysis took over the task of understanding the whole subject not only his conscious nature.

We can move on now to examine the dream as the medium that allows the *I* and *me* to face each other, complement each other and as a prototype of the links that constitute the dynamics of the intrapsychic. We can move on to learn about a subtle but intriguing outcome of the subject's duality: the wish. Only the human subject is the creature who can wish, and is unable to act upon a stimulus before turning it first into a wish.

Chapter Five

The Psychology of the Wish

The Wish as the Prototype of the Psyche

The philosophers' accomplishments that led to the birth of psychoanalysis were revealing a wish to find out a way to give their findings the perspective of a theory. It is uncanny that psychoanalysis, which was their extension, started by discovering the psychology of the wish. It is uncanny because the psychology of the wish came in the context of the subject's states of mind, which he has no conscious will to identify a wish in it. The wish seemed to depict the core of what is subjective about the subject: what he does not know about himself. What did psychoanalysis discover about the human subject to justify considering him the subject matter of its theory.

I mentioned in the introduction of the book, that Freud's endeavors were all geared toward finding the comprehensive functional theory that could explain his discoveries in the framework of causes and effects. He did not reach his objective because psychical phenomena, in essence, are reflections of the psychodynamics of the intrapsychic core of the subject. The intrapsychic is a 'structure' that relates to other structures that speak for the human subject. Dreams as wish fulfilment is a functional theory of cause (wish) and effect (dream). But a dream as the works of the three primary processes of condensation, displacement, and representability of ideas is a structural understanding of dreams. It deals with dreams as psychical structures of specific quality decided by the nature of the dream itself. At this point I have to digress and emphasize that structuralism was not known or yet appeared in the intellectual fielded during Freud's time. Therefore, Freud is not to blame for his functionalistic theorizing. On the contrary, although structuralism was not even on the horizon, all Freud's discoveries about the subject were structuralist in nature, although his theorizing was functional inform.

The insight that a physical symptom could express a psychical conflict and a psychical conflict (Freud, 1915c) could express a physical symptom is a structural outlook of the subject. So, the problem we have to solve is how to deal with structural insights and intuitions that were theorized by Freud functionally.

The human subject does not, even cannot, respond to the demands of external or internal stimuli directly. He first creates in 'his' mind a psychical representation of the stimulus which replaces the original stimulus that is demanding a response. He creates from the demand states of wishing that precedes the direct or immediate response. The fleeting pause between being stimulated and responding to the representation of the stimuli gives the response a personal subjective quality. This feature exists, even in the mentally retarded subjects, though in a less active and differentiating degree. This feature is solely human. Some animals respond in complicated manners to some stimuli, which suggest some active mental processing. However, because all members of their species respond in the same way to the same stimulation, we should obviate the notion of subjectivity in their behavior. They differ from other species but they do not show the personal nature which characterizes human responses.

Humans differ according to the individual mental and psychological endowment because of the psychical life that echoes each one's own consciousness. We react to the physical world with the dynamics of our intrapsychic world. The subject creates from the internal demands a state of wishing that precedes the direct or immediate reaction. This distinction between an instinctual response and a *Triebhaft* response decides the nature of theorizing about each. Generally speaking, theorizing is decided by the intention behind theorizing: explaining the phenomena or interpreting them. The subject matter of a theory of the subject, by virtue of its subject matter, has to be a theory of interpretation and not of explanations because explanations deal with the link between causes and 'their' effects and they could only be right or wrong. Interpretations, on the other hand deal with a latent meaning in the given manifest. Getting hungry creates the wish to eat and that wish will imply what is wanted and what is refused to eat too. The subject's issues stem from his dual nature, thus some of its aspects would not be there in its manifested display, and the latent will require some work to get to. Better, anything human is a duality of something conscious and something unconscious (not spontaneously available to the subject's mind but not necessarily repressed). Therefore, a theoretician in psychoanalysis should aspire to make the subject or other means to reveal the latent in the phenomenon he is trying to theorize about to complete the picture.

Psychoanalysis was the first methodical attempt at building such theory about the subject, thus continued the achievements of the philosophers. Theories of the subject based on functional explanations, like Adler's

'Individual Psychology,' offer explanations but are unsuccessful in making the subject understandable. Adler's notion of inferiority and superiority as fundamentals in individual psychology explains a psychological condition, but does not explain the subject himself who is caught within that duo of comparison. Freud tried that approach, but he was regularly disappointed in his efforts. His ambition did not blind him from seeing that he had already started building another kind of theory of the subject founded on the processes that start intrapsychically and determined by the nature and duality (Fayek, 2010)[1]. Most analysts still aspire to achieve that functional theory, or somehow believe that what they know is sort of the things that have proper independent psychical existence. Blass articulated this frustration well when he said, "Freud was convinced that his work led him to discover realities that lay beyond the directly observed data. Strangely, those who labeled Freud a positivist do not regard his realism to be contradictory to the alleged positivism, but rather as further evidence of it" (2002, p. 45).

Thinking in Functional and Structural Theories

Serious theoretical thinking would reveal something more profound in regard to the theory of the subject. Functional theories are based on deductive thinking. The theoretician deduces from what is apparent in the phenomenon the possible causes of it happening. In structural theories, like the proposed theory of the subject as it is supposed to be, the theoretician deals with phenomena that have part of the cause present but not sufficient to explain the whole phenomenon (see chapter ten). The reason is the impossibility of having in consciousness all the elements of a human phenomenon. There are three basic aspects of a human phenomenon that contribute to its formation, its cause, its effect, and the link between them, of which one of them, at least has to be unconscious. In the humanities, and psychoanalysis is a human science, the theorist has to go through a process of *induction* to reach the link between the partially obvious as cause and its partially clear effect to find the absent link in the phenomenon. For instance: the social scientist has to examine marriage as an effect, and social structuring as cause in order to reach the link

---

[1] Most psychoanalysts make the mistake of giving explanations for the patient's material, confusing explanations with interpretation (Traumata. Deprivation, etc.). Explanations are dead ends that would not encourage associating freely about their issues. Interpretations are elucidations of the patient's association that show the gap between the causes and their effect, thus encourage further association to fill that gap.

between them. Since marriage is a social organization that is different between societies but exists in all of them, the sociologist has to conclude – by inductive thinking – that the various modalities of marriage that exist in all societies serve one common but undeclared purpose. He will eventually realize that all societies have taboos of incest, which makes marriage a system of regulating social kinships to preserve each society's taboo.

The interpretations the psychoanalyst reaches by inductive thinking will reveal the particular structure of the phenomenon and not its cause. In the example given, sociologist-psychoanalyst will be able to interpret 'marriage' as defense against incest, regardless of the system of blood relations. A clinical psychoanalyst would work on a phobia to interpret the distorted meaning given to the phobic situation or object. Freud encountered several of those moments where 'deduction' failed making any contribution to understating a phenomenon. However, he 'inductively' discovered the nature of the link between the manifest dream and its latent content in the *Irma* dream, for instance. When he free-associated about the parts of the *Irma* dream to find its meaning, he did not discover the meaning but discovered the workings of the primary process, instead. Freud's deductions, which were not a few, did not add to psychoanalysis much. His intuitions, which were not many but were always timely, had the mark of inductive thinking, i.e., not discovering realities but uncovering the missing essence of the established realities. He approached the gap between the manifest content of the latent dream meaning as a structural gap; not something missing that is caused by external factors to the dreaming process itself but as an implicit meaning in what is evident. What could have made him realize that his intuition was the interpretation of the dream; and made him celebrate the moment and the place he got it.

Another intuition was that the dream is instigated by a wish aroused in the day before the dream happened; but the recent wish has to get support from a similar infantile wish to initiate the dream. In the *Irma* dream, the wish to exonerate himself of making a wrong diagnosis was not enough to create the dream, because it did not provide the way he could dream-work that exoneration. The total victory over all his nemeses in the dream came from a childhood situation when the childhood wish did not have censorship on its megalomaniac limits. Thus, the dream process gets started when the wish gets the way to be fulfilled from the power of a childhood wish. Although the idea of a wish from the day before the night of the dream is a sensible thing to consider, the idea of a duo of wishes of which one is from childhood is mindboggling to come from deductive thinking. The intuition is a model of the inductive process of thinking that characterizes intuitions.

Freud was 'destined' to reverse the prevailing approach to studying the human subject. All attempts before him were starting from learning more about the subject's attributes to finally get to his true nature (deduce it). He started from understanding the subject to restructuring his nature. This is a reasonable way to look at psychoanalysis as a human science, and not a theory of 'something.' Every structural revelation Freud had about the subject (a wishing subject) initiated changes to the concept of the subject and required advancing his research to catch up with those new revelations. The wish and the state of wishing changed the subject from being impelled by drives to being impelled by *Trieben*. Infantile sexuality was possible to consider only with the concept of *Trieb*[2] being the driving force behind the psychical phenomena. This different outlook on the subject was the start of a psychoanalytic way of understanding the subject. It is important to note that the clinical psychoanalyst to consider every psychoanalytic discovery a force of change to our conception of ourselves and pushes us further ahead because our contemporary subject is not the same that was at Freud's time.

Dreams and Wish Fulfillment

---

[2] Strachey's unfortunate translation of the German term *Trieb* by the English instinct objectified the process of the response to an endosomatic source, and ignored the subjectivity of human responses. The result of that seems minor but it changes all psychical phenomena to objects looking for nouns (drive psychology). Instinct is a term applies to animal behaviour denoting reaction to a need or demand by innate, typical, unlearned, and direct response to that need. Thus, it deserved to be identified as drive and naming its denotation; like a drive to eat or to copulate, etc. Freud chose the German *Trieb* for human motivations, although the term *Instink* exists in German, because human responses to stimulation are an individual and a subjective matter. It is never totally the same. *Trieb* denotes the process behind our responses, and has no proper translation in other languages (Freud, 1926 e). It denotes a demand put on the mind to respond to a stimulus. The significance of that distinction is putting the emphasis on the specificity of human reactions. The subject does not respond to the stimulus itself, but to a representation that becomes a demand put on the mind to act. This subtle difference (or maybe not so subtle) proposes that the human subject does not reacts to physical demands (drives) but to what happens mentally to the physical pressure the stimulus puts on the mind. The pause between stimulation and responding to its representation transforms the stimulus into a wish. The subject does not respond to hunger by eating; he responds to transforming hunger into a wish to eat, then comes the act of eating with all the variations it takes.

The birth of psychoanalysis came with interpreting dreams (*The Interpretation of Dreams, 1900a*). The discovery of the primary and secondary processes, dream work, the nature of interpretation, and the contribution of childhood psychical life to the creation of the intrapsychic life of the adult subject, were all there 'existing' in the dream and dream interpretation. However, the real appreciation of dreams and dream interpretation came back to psychoanalysis long after neglecting its early discovery.

The Interpretation of Dreams (Freud, 1900a) deals more with the processes that characterize the subject than merely being a text on dreams. In that work Freud was – indirectly – working on the duality of the *I* and *me*, and the active *I* (the dreamer, the patients, the joking person, etc.) versus the observing *I*, which perceives and talks about his psychological creations. The '*Irma* dream' was the first personal attempt at discovering the dreamer's intention to dream. The dream proved that each part of it is a statement that generates a different chain of association which links with the other chains, i.e. the dream, in the final analysis, is one statement formulated by the dreamer to express one of his thoughts. In that dream, Freud was saying that he did not make a mistake in the diagnosis of Irma, but someone else caused the deterioration in her condition. More or less, the dream exonerated him from shame and fulfilled his wish to vindicate himself. He realized from interpreting the dream, and the dreams of others, that dreams could reveal the repressed (counterpart). This simple deduction meant that one could listen to his own counterpart speaking to him if his dreams were interpreted to him (Fayek, 1980). This was the first intuition of a general psychoanalytic significance. He decided to work on the gap between the subject awake and his-self asleep in order to understand dreaming and to reveal differences between the languages that separate the *I* from *me*.

Interpreting dreams might look insignificant now in regard to a general psychoanalytic theory, because it was followed by further and more interesting discoveries, which seem now more important. Point in fact; interpreting dreams was just a step toward all other discoveries. The epithet 'a dream is a wish fulfilled' is important, but only if the accent is put on the 'wish' and not on the 'fulfilment' in the dream. *Fulfilling wishes in dreams reveals something about wishes more than about dreams.* This is what made Freud consider dream interpretation one of the two most important discoveries of psychoanalysis. Dreams uncovered the way to decipher and understand symptoms too and practically other human phenomena that were not part of the analytic field yet. He stated this idea in a letter to Fliess (January 3, 1899) saying: "I will only reveal to you that the dream-pattern is capable of the most general application that the key to hysteria as well really lies in dreams... If I wait a little longer, I shall be able to describe the mental processes in dreams in such a way that it also includes the process in the formation of hysterical symptoms." He believed that his interpretation of dreams is bridging the gap between the subject (conscious) and the counterpart (unconscious). He also had the notion that dream interpretation will show how to bridge the gap between a theory of the human subject and a theory of psychopathology. He said (1900a): "It is my intention to make use of my present elucidation of dreams as a preliminary step toward solving the more di cult problems of the psychology of the neuroses" (p. 104). The notion of looking in the normal processes (dreams) for the nature of psychopathology (hysteria) reversed the direction he took in an important previous work. In the 'Project' (1950a), he intended to use neurology to build a psychology and ended up with a psychology for neurologists.

The gap between the subject and his counterpart had to wait for a new intuition to discover what could make each recognize the other. Freud noticed very early in working with hysterical patients that symptoms *say* something, unintentionally or unconsciously, on behalf of the counterpart (the case of Katharina, 1895b). Freud wanted to learn the language of the unconscious *me*, so he could translate it to the conscious *I*. This was a very important aspect of Freud's intuitive gift: he wanted the subject to learn from himself how to listen and understand what his counterpart is unconsciously saying. The notion that the patient learns in his analysis how it is done is an important part of psychoanalytic therapy. He concluded that he should learn the language of the counterpart in the normal person first and then see how it could apply to patients. It is imperative to note here that the steps Freud took to discover anything about psychoanalysis are almost accidental and not deliberate. We should pay attention to how Freud was immersed in looking for the etiology and causality of hysteria in the early phase of his clinical practice, and then suddenly he concluded that: "actually, a satisfactory general understanding of neuro-psychotic disturbance is not possible unless one can make a connection with clear presuppositions about normal psychical processes" (1897a).

This was a major part of his insights and the breakthrough in dealing with most of the problem in psychoanalysis. He sensed – indirectly – that we need a theory of the subject in order for any theory of psychopathology of the person could be reached and acquire significance.

There is an understated Freudian intuition about the fulfilled wish in the dream, which was actually instrumental in starting the psychoanalytic discovery as whole. Two years before the coining of the famous statement of a dream is wish fulfillment, Freud said (1900 a): "It seems to me that the theory of wish fulfillment has brought up only the psychological solution and not the biological [metapsychological]. Biologically, dream-life seems to me derives entirely from the residues of the pre-historic period of life (between the ages of one and three) – the same period, which is the source of the unconscious and alone contains the etiology of all psychoneuroses...[A] recent wish only leads to a dream if it can put itself in connection with material from this prehistoric period, if a recent wish is a derivative of a prehistoric one, or can get itself adopted by one" (274, fn. 5). This insight of the psychology of the wish underlines two important points that we would encounter in any future theory of the subject. The first is that the duality of what is recent and what is older (in wishes) reveals that the subject's duality is not regarding oppositions of things like *Cs.-Ucs.*, libido-aggression, sexual *Trieb*-ego *Trieb*, childhood-adulthood, etc., those are not dualities; they are opposites, because they share and are degrees of the same basic quality. Duality is created by a process that makes an entity 'divide' into antitheses, i.e. they coexist making the nature of the human subject an unstable issue. They are not 'doubles' in conflict where one annuls the other, they are dualities in a complementarity.

The second point is considering keeping in mind, all the time, that the subject is the originator of all those features, both as processes and things. Therefore, we are not analyzing 'something psychological' but something that pertains to a particular subject. In other terms, psychoanalysts do not interpret dreams but the dreams of the subjects they are listening to. To put this point in an understandable clinical way: psychoanalysis does not make the unconscious conscious but activates in the subject the process that turns the unconscious into consciousness. This means that the duality of *I-me* is a duality of my *me* as a child and *I* as the adult dreamer.

Earlier to dream interpretation Freud suggested that hysterical patients suffer from reminiscences and strangulation of emotions (Breuer and Freud, 1895 b). This was a functional theory of hysterical symptoms in which they were treated to 'discovered' causes. His first attempt at dealing with dreams resulted in another functional statement. This kind of reductionist thinking could have tempted Freud to abandon his insights very early, because they sounded as if psychoanalysis was going to be a theory of things. His deductive thinking stopped at points where he felt a need to change direction and attitude, especially in the way he posed his questions. For instance, he noticed on his own that every psychological theory, apart from what is achieved from the point of view of natural science, must fulfill yet another major requirement; it has to "explain to us what we are aware of in the most puzzling fashion, through our consciousness. Since this consciousness knows nothing of what we have so far been assuming quantities of neurons – it should explain this lack of knowledge to us as well" (1950 a, 307–308). Fortunately, Freud noticed very early that a psychological theory is fundamentally different from other theories that pertain to objects because a theory of the subject is a conscious formulation of unconscious components. He changed the question from what things should a psychological theory explain to what is the psychological theory that could explain those things we deal with? Further, he changed the question from what are the attributes of the subject that a psychological theory should be dealing with, to what is the psychological theory that could deal with the human subject and his attributes? (Elder, 1994, p. 179).

The Interpretation of Wish

Freud's discovery of meaning in dreams is seldom considered beyond its statement: "A dream is wish fulfillment." However, the notion of wish fulfillment was only the beginning of his work on dreams, and the rest of *The Interpretation of Dreams* was the unfolding of that starting point. He was able through his work on the wish and dreams to change the concept of the unconscious and keep changing it till he came to its tripartite nature: the dynamic, the topographic, and systemic (Freud, 1915c). What was originally called 'the repressed' proved to be a discovery of the subject's way of dealing with something he wishes, and just wants casually. All living subjects encounter moments when they lack something, and they sense a 'want' for that thing. The subject's duality creates a gap between sensing the lack and becoming conscious of it in order to act upon getting it. The state of wishing is a unique condition in homosapiens because it changes from childhood to maturity, differs from subject to subject, is also sensitive to cultural and other social factors, and reveals many unconscious factors that relate to its initiation and the way the subject will deal with it. The state of wishing – as the onset of consciousness in the sense of being – is the focus of many transformations. The most common and also interesting is the transformation from wishing to desiring.

Wishing, although it is simply a manifestation of the duality of being conscious, is a step before acting. It does not stop at that. A state of wishing creates an important place and role for the 'other' in the process of its fulfillment. The place of the other in wishing is the earliest of the infant's experience, because the fulfillment of the wish requires the presence of the other, which has a major role in affecting his sense of self. The infant's wishes are fulfilled by the presence of the other in every wishing state. Whatever the wish or the age and time of its happening, it will always create another for it to be fulfilled (even a fantasmic other). The most important part in this transformation is the other's own desire to fulfill the subject's wish. There is a major difference between the infant's wish to feed if it is met by a mother who wants to feed rather than a reluctant feeding mother. Therefore, wishes transform and become desires when the other is recognized and considered essential in fulfilling them. Clinically speaking, the other is either a real desiring other, or a permissive counterpart.

This feature in the subject explains another important one that is central in the dynamics of the intrapsychic. A wish is an event that could expire after its fulfilment. On the other hand, a desire does not expire, because of its links with the desires of the other. A desiring mother fulfilling the infant's desires establishes a lasting relationship with the infant. Desire is a process that creates a complex psychological structure. The relationship between one's desire and the desires of others is a major element in the intrapsychic life of the subject. Our clinical experience presents us with the complexities of the links between the patient's own desires and the exchanges with the desires of the others; including the desire to fulfill his desire. The psychoanalytic situation allows the history of desiring to be re-enacted in the transference.

The Interpretation of Dreams (1900a) suggests that Freud started his theory of dreams with three assumptions (principles) and succeeded in proving them. The clearest and the first is that dreams have meaning and are not, as previously thought, merely psychical reactions caused by external or internal stimuli (Freud,1900 a, chapter one). He did not start with dreams looking for interpretations, but with propositions that could be supported if interpreting dreams is possible. Better, he did not have a clear idea of the act of interpretation (it was still in the works of his clinical work), but it dawned on him to apply it to dreams. The second assumption stipulates that the meaning of dreams that comes from an interpretation could reveal the process by which it was hidden, or the manner by which that process has worked out a way to hide it. The third assumption is that revealing the process behind the formation of dreams (uncovering the workings of that process) would be the natural way to bridge the gap between the manifest and the latent, and between the subject and his counterpart.

Freud's intuition came to him while attempting to interpret a dream of his own. He said (1900a): "the meaning of the dream was borne in upon me. I became aware of an intention which was carried into e ect by the dream and which must have been my motive for dreaming it. The dream fulfilled certain wishes which were started in me by the events of the previous evening. The conclusion of the dream, that is to say, was that I was not responsible for the persistence of Irma's pains, but it was Otto…The dream represented a particular state of a airs as I should have wished it to be. Thus, its content was the fulfilment of a wish and its motive was a wish" (ibid, p.118–119). This first completely interpreted dream, proved three points: (I) a dream is simply a direct presentation of a situation happening in the present tense. (II) When a dream is interpreted, it reveals an already fulfilled wish (ibid. 119). (III) The residues of the day before the dream could explain the dream content (the manifest dream) and shed light on the motive behind that particular dream. But the fulfilled wish in any dream is neither part of the manifest dream nor the associations of the dream; it is an 'inductive find' that comes from the link between both of them. The wish, which interprets the dream as a psychical event, is obtained inductively not deductively. Freud generalized that all dreams were wish fulfillments, creating a theory regarding the structuring of dreams and his theory of the workings of the primary process ended all previous functional theories of dreams, and also paved the way for a general tendency to note structuralism even before its inception in the thirties of the century.

This shift needs further exploration, because it calls into question the dream as a function of a wish seeking fulfilment. If Freud's wish in the *Irma* dream was to exonerate himself of making a bad diagnosis, he did not feel such fulfillment while dreaming, nor was that wish present in any form in the manifest dream. It came to his mind when he was awake, 'watching his dream.' Politzer (1994) said, "If the dream, and in general the neurotic symptoms, have a meaning, they have this meaning at the time they are produced; and if the dream in particular is the satisfaction of a desire [wish] it is this satisfaction at the moment it is dreamed" (p. 119). *What does it mean, then, that a dream is a wish fulfillment if the wish is neither there in the fabric of the manifest dream nor in the latent content, but only shows itself in the work of interpretation?* Still, Otto's bad news about the patient Irma was the day residue that aroused in Freud more than the wish to exonerate himself, but also the wish to accuse Irma of causing her own misery, which shows in her behavior in the dream. A dream, then, could fulfill more than one wish. *Could that be the root of the phenomenon of the after-effect (Freud, 1918b)?*

The existence of another process behind the formation of dreams caught Freud's attention. He noticed something unconscious in the emergence of meaning in the dream, but only while interpreting the dream. It was an inductive thought. Freud had a vague notion of that process in the 'Project' (1950a). He said there that "there is something beyond our perception, which we can still only describe with the vocabulary of perception and conception, and despite its independence, it will remain unknowable" (ibid, pp. 196–197). He did not assume, until then, that the unconscious was something that existed behind the wish fulfillment. It is peculiar that as Freud inferred an unconscious element form dream interpretation, he was able to move from the functional explanation of dreams to explaining the structural nature of the wish, i.e., dreams present the dreamer's wish as already fulfilled. Freud's examination of wishes in dreams (more than fifty of his own and one hundred and fifty of others') made him less emphatic about the wish-fulfillment formula he proposed at the beginning. He said that (1900 a): "dreams are given their shape…by the operation of two forces: and that one of the forces constructs the wish…while the other exercises a censorship upon this dream-wish" (144). Surprisingly, Freud later added a footnote to this statement (in the 1930a edition) saying, "a dream [may] expresses a wish of the second agency," meaning that some dreams could be the fulfillment of the wish to censor another wish (p. 146). This sudden change in direction divested the dream wish of any permanent quality, thus it should be considered as a condition or a state that derives its quality from the system that produces it. In other words, it is *wishing not the wish, as such, that creates dreams*. Wishing is the unconscious process of dreaming, as well as its structural characteristic.

In that early stage of discovering the unconscious Freud dealt with the dream as a symptomatic event, not as a natural phenomenon. It was about a subject who has unacceptable wishes – as in psychoneuroses – and when asleep and his 'censorship' is weakened he dreams; he dreams of fulfilling those 'sick' wishes. Thus, it is not the wish that creates the dream; on the contrary, dreaming as a psychological activity recalls what was the dreamer frustrated by (in the day residue), and provides it with the scene of fulfillment. The dream is not a wish fulfillment but wish fulfillment is the force behind dreaming as a psychical phenomenon. The wish was seen as an experience of frustration that required the subject to deal with, regardless of what system generates the dream, daydream, symptom, fantasy, etc.

We have to note Freud's insight that the wish of the day residue requires a wish from childhood to give it the impetus to create a dream is totally inductive. There is also no obvious reason to justify this modification of the previous formula. However, separation of the wish of the day residue from the childhood wish was implicitly separating wishing from the wish itself, and relating wishing to the *Ucs*. As such, it was possible to look at dreams as products of impulses (causes to be identified) and also as representations of impulses (texts to be interpreted), thus dreaming is an essential feature of the subject's psychological state. In the analysis of the dream of The Burning Child (1900a, 509–511) Freud identified two very obvious features in all dreams that when added to the previous argument they verify an important aspect in the theory of the subject. Freud said about that dream: "Two almost independent features stand out as characteristic of the form taken by this dream. One was the fact that the thought is represented as an immediate situation with the 'perhaps' omitted, and the other is the fact that the thought is transformed into a visual image and speech" (ibid, 534). The first feature of using only the present tense, which is also the tense of daydreaming and fantasies, makes the wish a statement that has no commentary on the event (I wish says nothing about the time of the wish, but could mention the one wishing). The second feature is transforming thoughts into sensory images, which are experienced with a high level of conviction of their reality. The two features indicate that 'wishing' is a spontaneous psychical state that is not conditional on any particular frustration, deprivation, time, or history. Better, since there is no end for wishing as a human condition, and there is no total satisfaction that ends all wishing, the subject lives a present that always comes from a time before the formation of any wish that has a definite existence in consciousness.

The Wish and Its Antithesis

There are some characteristics of dreams and symptoms that are to be identified. Dreams and symptoms – maybe all other psychical phenomena – are timeless, eventless, if not even contentless. We do not dream only when we have wishes that are nagging us. We also develop neurotic symptoms that are not related to certain difficulties we experience (they actually create difficulties and are not the outcome of difficulties). Dreams, character formations, and symptoms are there in every subject all the time; they only say something in the present time and about the present time although they always come from periods in past. They are also captured in a sensory form, which the subject has to verbalize, or at least understand in his non-verbal form. A person's exhibitionism, for instance, is always there waiting for the occasion to be acted out. Psychical phenomena –regardless of the circumstances – are always lived as if they were new. They never say anything about the past as past, only of the past as a previous experience similar to the present one. They are the story of the present, and proffer nothing of the future. Those two features are unusual compared to the natural daily events of waking life. The wish that is fulfilled in a dream could be a product of any of the three psychical systems (ego, id, superego). Thus, the wish of the dream has no typical quality; it is not predicated on any 'specifics.' Since neither the nature nor the source of the wish is essential to create or activate it, we cannot say that the dream is wish fulfillment as such, unless we overlook that a wish does not have a specific entity. We could only say that the fulfillment of any wish, even in waking life, takes the form and acquires the state of dreaming; it happens in a dreamlike fashion. Symptoms convey wishful thinking, and in their final analysis they are structured like dreams, or by the same process that structures dreams (Freud 1916–1917a).

The other point is that a wish does not generate in consciousness the exact signs of its existence, because it is contentless. Nonetheless, it does that in a disguised manner, as in symptoms or dreams. If we face a psychological act that denotes an active wish, we should know that that is because the wish in that act was in conflict with its antithesis or the anti-wish. The wish is always in conflict with another force working against it (censorship) but not an opposite wish. The wish in Freud's own conception of dreams was not the core of dreams; the psychology of wishing was that core. He said (1900 a) that the dream-content is "not a faithful translation or a point-by-point projection of dream thoughts, but a highly incomplete and fragmentary version of them" (281). This conclusion strongly suggests that a wish in the dream creates its own opposition through the impetus of the duality of the subject. The conflict in the dream is not between two wishes, but within one and the same wish. Blass said (2002): "What Freud considered to be his revelation was that he could discover the actual connections in the mind that were responsible for the appearance of dreams – the actual connections that were finding expression through it…the actual connections that exist within the mind" (p. 49).

Freud's further understanding of dream-work identified three main workings in that operation: 1. condensation, 2. displacement, 3. pictorial representation of ideas. Condensation showed itself in the interpretation of Irma's dream, where Irma stood for and represented several other characters in a condensed way (Freud, 1900 a, pp. 292–293). Metaphor is the linguistic attribute of condensation (Cassirer, 1953), thus Irma's case was the metaphor of the threat to the dreamer's integrity. The next operation of displacement is linguistically metonymy (ibid). In dreams those two linguistic attributes function di erently than in our waking life, because in dreams, we do not purposely use them to express more than what we have in mind. Metaphors and metonymies muddle up the manifest content of the dream (and symptoms) and distort the expression of the wish. That happens just by the way the primary process utilizes them. Their e ect on the manifest dream is what Freud called censorship. Censorship is a residual concept of the outdated cathartic theory in which all psychical phenomena were pathological and leaned toward hiding from consciousness. Yet, metaphor and metonymy are constituents of our natural linguistic expressions (verbal and nonverbal) and the foundation of the regular way of 'saying' things about things. They are – par excellence – the prerequisites of the subject's duality, because without this verbal facility we could not have had any means to relate to the other through our different desires. The third work of the dream-work is "the means for pictorial representation." The only medium available in sleep for the psyche to perform is the availability of pictorial expressing. A wish demanding recognition has to find the other who reads the wish and turns it into a desire. There is no other means to express desires except by pictorially 'showing' it as fulfilled wish. Dreams are very suitable for that. It is intriguing how the notion of the dream as wish fulfillment is derived from those two dream mechanisms: always in the present tense and in a pictorial form. Freud said that a dream has no alternative but to present the wish as being fulfilled because it has no sense of time except the present time (1900a, p. 235, Blanco, 1975). Those attributes are well fitted to describing daydreams too, which are the conscious equivalent of fantasies in the neuroses.

However, dreams "have no means at their disposal for presenting, logical relations between the dream-thoughts. The restoration of the connections which the dream-work has destroyed is a task which has to be performed by the interpretative process" (ibid, p. 312)3. Freud displayed an unusual inductive ability in finding the grammatical rules that guide the dream in dealing with concepts like *if, when, un-, and, after etc.* In other words, if a wish has to borrow a form in order to be expressed, then a dream has no other means to express that wish except by pictorially presenting it, showing it as a fulfilled event. Wittgenstein (1982) said, "The representation of a wish is, eo ipso, the representation of its fulfilment" (pp. 64–65). In fact, the dream fulfills wishes by virtue of its capability of representing them as realized and actualized. What makes the dream a wish fulfillment is the facility of representation more than the content of the wish.

The wish and its antithesis in the dream (and symptom) are framed by the interplay of primary and secondary processes. Freud expressed this seemingly insignificant part of the dream-work by saying: "The dream-thoughts and the dream-content are presented to us like two versions of the same subject matter in two di erent languages. Or, more appropriately, the dream-content seems like a transcript of the dream-thought into another mode of expression, whose characters and syntactic laws it is our business to discover by comparing the original and the translation" (1900a, p. 277). The notion of dream-language had far-reaching implications because it meant that a dream should be treated as a statement or a text written in a special language, which requires translation, i.e., interpretation to get to its meaning.

From this exposition of the psychology of the wish it is easy, if not logical, to see that the psychology of the wish is the psychology of the intrapsychic. Wishes split into dualities; each is amenable to any content, resulting into conflicts, not belonging to a 'specific' but to a sense of lack that relate to each other within the dynamics of the primary and secondary processes.

Chapter Six
Sexuality and the Trieb (Instinct)

The scientific rigor of the discoveries in physical sciences is obvious and could be assessed independently of the results themselves. This is not a feature of the human sciences. Discoveries in the human sciences give the impression of being random, disjointed, undirected, and almost uncertain. One explanation is that human nature is not similar to physical nature, which is stable and predictable. However, there is another reason that is not easy to consider because proving it comes retrospectively, after the fact. Discoveries in the field of the humanities look as if they are dormant issues that are waiting for some gifted person to have the intuition of their existence. This is true – to a great extent – because human phenomena like sex are complex configurations that defy any attempt at itemizing them to study each item separately. Learning about the subject is predetermined by factors that could only be grasped retroductively. For instance, Schopenhauer and Hegel were responding to the implicit questions in Descartes's Cogito. Their intuitions stimulated the intuitive process in other thinkers like Freud and guided him to the notions of the *unconscious counterpart*. Therefore, we cannot predict or anticipate what we will discover next regarding the subject.

The psychology of the wish reveals an attribute of the subject that could explain why sexuality was – figuratively speaking – the spark that set psychoanalysis ablaze. The nature of the wish is to change into a desire, and desires involve the other to be gratified. The mother is the primal 'other' that will impress her nature on every gratification of desire that will follow. This everlasting impact comes from the early-and mostly only-experience in the building of the intrapsychic core of the subject. The infantile 'wish-desire' activates a *Trieb* structure. By this I mean that the infant will reactivate – later in life – the representation of the object of his wish and will repeat the process of relating to that representation.

All social relations begin with a wish (of a *Trieb* structure) leading to a desire which makes the relation with the other 'objects' a dynamic scene of the intrapsychic. The psychology of the wish gives *Trieb* the leading role in relating to the other, with all the subjective variations implicated in those relations. This is a major differential attribute that is characteristic of the human subject. Sex in homosapiens is the prototype of a wish turned into a desire that implicates the other because of the conscious awareness of the role of the other (chosen) in the pleasure gained in the sexual act. Sex, psychologically considered in humans, is not instinctual.

Discovering the fallacy of a well-established idea (belief) and venturing to defying it, the fallacy of a common idea becomes more interesting, even intriguing, when it happens to the same thinker, because he becomes his own stimulator to venture and defies himself. This self-provoking process happened to Freud several times due to the demand for a theory of the subject. Freud's interest in the nature of consciousness and the discovery of the unconscious led him to his first misleading theory of repression and sexuality. This discovery came by in the 'interpretation of dreams' and Freud found himself (unconsciously) understanding the psychology of the wish. Things were not the same after the psychology of the wish; it was like the plug in Aladdin's lamp. Once Freud unplugged the lamp of psychoanalysis it was (and still is) impossible to bring the Genie back in. Jones once asked Freud about his most favorite work. Freud specifically pointed at the book on dreams and the book on sexuality (Jones 1954, p. 384). He added that it was his *destiny* to discover the most banal things: dreams have a meaning and sexuality exists in children from the beginning. Freud said that a theory of sexuality might be the next work after *The Interpretation of Dreams* (Masson, 1985). A few months later, he wrote to him again saying: "I am collecting material for the theory of sexuality and waiting for a spark to set the accumulated material on fire" (Masson, 1985). It took five more years for that spark to ignite the publication of the *Three Essays on the Theory of Sexuality*, but the link between the book on the wish and the book on infantile sexuality proved to be a lasting link; they sparked the fire that was psychoanalysis itself.

The book on sexuality introduced the concept of *Trieb* (translated by instinct and sometimes by drive). *Trieb* was a concept that enabled Freud to account for the variations and versatility of sexuality. He firmly changed an old conception by stating that sexuality is not limited to genital intercourse but is the pleasure that accompanies that act. He added that such pleasure could be obtained from other physical activities and other organs than the sexual ones. We encounter in that choice of terms something that he fleetingly recognized in the psychology of the wish: it is *not the wish that counts but the state of wishing.* Freud's view on sexuality, as his on the wish, freed psychoanalysis from dealing with issues, subjects, entities, etc. and confirmed that it deals with processes that encompass those topics. The connection between wish and sexuality is not a connection of two issues that could be envisaged or tried; it shows *Freud's way of thinking: he noticed and conceived of the connections between them, not as accidental but as predetermined.* The book on dreams proved to be on wishing and not on dreams, and the book on sexuality also proved to be more on *Trieb* and not on sex.

Sex constitutes a demand put on the mind to act upon it. The connection between the two issues of wish (or desire) and sexuality is in the initiation of acting upon the mental representations of those two demands. A theory of the subject is a theory of those kinds of connections and links. Freud's conception of the subject's dealings with his internal and external stimulation makes the *Trieb* a precondition for all state of wishing.

Sex as Trieb

After a number of years of making sexuality the source of all psychopathologies Freud reversed the cliché and strived instead to investigate and explain the psychoneuroses to explain sexuality. This shift reminds of the shift from the content of the wish and its possible repression if objectionable to wishing as the structural nature of dreams. However, Freud turning the issue of sexuality upside down was different from the way he did with the wish. Sexuality in the first etiological theory was the cause of the psychoneuroses in adults. Introducing infantile sexuality and adding sexual phantasies to sexuality became a function of the psychoneuroses and no longer considered the structure of the neuroses. In other words, *he shifted the accent from the patient's sexual experiences – as cause of his neuroses – to the patient's specific psychoneurosis as the cause of his particular sexual life*[1]. Furthermore, at the time when Freud was introducing his theory of sexuality to the professional world, sexuality was considered a sign of biological maturation, which prompts the mutual attraction of mature members of the opposite sexes. Their attraction was thought to be mainly aimed at the union between the person and the object of his sexual attraction. But, with a place for infantile sexuality in the maturation process, it became a process that starts from the beginning and does not just happen in puberty.

---

[1] This shift is would be in harmony with psychoanalysis as the science of the subject's intrapsychic core.

This prevailing ordinary notion of sexuality conflicted with most of the commonly known sexual behaviors at his time. Sexuality displayed a wide variety of deviations from what was almost a hypothetical model. Those variations were – I believe – what Freud was collecting and awaiting the spark that would set them afire. He also proved – using sexual deviations in adults – that sexuality is not a mere desire that agrees or conflicts with the moral standards that are set up for its practice. It was a complex psychobiological construct. The new psychoanalytic theory of sexuality included sexual phantasies, which made it part of the psychological life of the subject. Infantile sexuality was made to account for a significant part of the link between sexuality and psychoneuroses, yet not in the old functional meaning. Infantile sexuality has become a basic component of the structural core of the psychological life of the subject and lost its luster as its cause.

For a while Freud set up a life *Trieb* as the antithesis of the sexual *Trieb*. Hence, sexuality lost is causative function to become just one of the sensitive aspects of the human subject's susceptibility to psychoneuroses. The period of the duality of sexuality vs. life preservation was a much better reformulation of the duality of sexual libido and vital libido, which he proposed before.

Psychoanalysis, at the beginning of the twentieth century, was a lively field of discoveries about the subject. It stimulated the fields of psychiatry, psychology, philosophy, and several other worthy intellectual initiatives. Some social events and more public responses to the new theory of sexuality initiated by psychoanalysis was a main contributor to that vitality. Its unique understanding of sexuality was the main stimulation in the Cultural Revolution of the twentieth century. Freud's theory of sexuality separated sex from morality, thus liberating the subject from a major hindrance in the way of understanding himself. Therefore, no theory of the subject would mean much without understanding Freud's theory of sexuality.

It is not clear if sexual deviations are what prompted Freud to study sexuality in children, or infantile sexuality was the eye opener to the origin of sexual deviations in adults. He noticed the separateness of the sexual *object* (the subject of the sexual wish) and the sexual *aim* (the sexual wish). This was a significant distinction which supported the notion that the sexual life of the human subject is radically different from its existence in the rest of the primates. Sex in the animal kingdom is a straightforward act that pertains to procreation and has only a biological predisposition for pleasure (sometimes it relates to issues of domination). Human sexuality shows very little and faint signs of its link to procreation, but reveals its involvement in most other aspect of pleasure, including what we get in social interactions. It contributes to other facets of life either as an act that has an aim or a proclivity toward an object.

Thus, the sexuality of the human subject is a duality like everything else in his nature. Freud added to his new discoveries another attribute: *sexuality is a function that matures with development – from infancy to adulthood – in a predetermined pattern that corresponds with stages in the maturity of physical needs*[2]. This feature is absent in sexuality in the animal kingdom, which gets activated physiologically by age and biological maturation. It remains the same with no signs of change since its activation. In infantile sexuality, the aims and objects are originally unlinked but get connected in the course of maturation. Freud's suggestion that sexuality in the human subject is 'delinked' from its physio-biological origin made him conclude (1905d): "Perhaps the sexual instinct itself may be no simple thing but put together from components which have come apart in the perversions. If this is so, the clinical observations of these abnormalities will have drawn our attention to amalgamations which have been lost to view in the uniform behavior of normal people" (162).

Despite this insight into the internal structure of sexuality Freud did not abandon – right away – his etiological theory of the psychoneuroses, in which they are functions of sexuality and its normality. He still maintained that there was some merit left in that etiology and said, "All my experience shows that these psychoneuroses are based on sexual instinctual forces. By this I mean that the energy of the sexual instinct [libido] makes a source of energy of the neurosis and that in consequence the sexual life of the person in question is expressed – whether exclusively or principally or only partially – in these symptoms" (ibid, 163). He tried repeatedly and in vain to give the sexual instinct, in its new perspective, a place within the etiology of the psychoneuroses by insisting on keeping the concept of the libido as the agent of explanations in psychoanalysis, because thus he can talk about sexuality without the restriction of it not being a drive.

Freud identified three constituents of a *Trieb* as instigators of psychical activity: *source* (pressure in a body part), *aim* (discharging of the pressure), and an *object* (through which the discharge happens). He differentiated *Trieb* from any other source of action-reaction by two things: 1. *Trieb* is a continuous source of stimulation from *within* (endosomatic, physiological demands, changes in homeostasis), contrasted with external sources of stimulation that comes from *without* (external physical world). 2. *Trieb* deals with the stimulus by representing it mentally (better psychically) first, before instigating any

---

[2] For some time in the history of psychoanalysis the psychosexual model of development was the guiding and effective framework of most its new discoveries. The interest in functional explication of psychoanalysis retired the psychosexual model of development.

particular action. In the human subject all somatic stimuli are changeable to mental representations, thus they are predisposed to becoming psychological stimulations. He said (1905d): "The simplest and likeliest assumption to the nature of *Trieb* would seem to be that in itself *an instinct is without quality*, and, so far as mental life is concerned, it is only to be regarded as a measure of the demand put on the mind to work" (168; italics added). *Trieb*, as *quality-less or contentment-less* entity, pertains to the physical bod where the endosomatic stimuli originate. The source of a *Trieb* varies according to the particular organ involved in the mental representation but it is always experienced as pressure that is missing the quality which would define it. Freud's elucidation of this point was very new and surprising. He was almost *talking of a state of wishing that needs an identity*. However, the shadow of pathology kept that distinction from reaching its full potential and clarity. The *source* of the *Trieb* was always just *pressure* (urge to act), which did not differ in its nature but differed in its *aim* and the corresponding *object* that could facilitate its discharge.

The pressure causes pain and the discharge generates pleasure. This was the point that made Freud call those parts of the body *erotogenic zones*, because they were parts or organs in the body where the *Trieb*'s pressure is felt as pain but were also centers of pleasure when the pressure was dealt with.

Freud's insight of infantile sexuality implied that the sexual *Trieb* does not have a static construct (not *Instinkt-instinct*), but a developing, evolving condition, hence its earlier forms play a role in its later organized mature stages. Moving from one erotogenic zone to the next forces the endosomatic stimulus of each zone to integrate with the stimuli of the previous stages and with their representations. Therefore, it acquires wider and richer attachments to the sexual objects and the external world as whole. By representing the endosomatic stimuli in the mind, the sexual *Trieb* achieves its aim in the most intriguing way: the representation functions as search light that discovers, creates, and gets attached to the objects that pave the way to satisfy that aim. *In an unusual clarification of the origins of psychical life, Freud (1933 a) said that the Trieb becomes psychically operating on its way from its source in the erotogenic zone to its object in the world, which gets satisfaction passing by the appropriate aim (Lecture 32).*

Those insights should have convinced Freud (but did not) that there is no sexual *Trieb*, but that sexuality is available – as content – for the *Triebhaft* nature of the subject's response to the internal and the external worlds. In other words, sexuality is not a qualification of the *Trieb*, but could become its content. Sexuality in that sense is the urge for representing the emerging power of the preservation and procreation of life. This is enough reason to stress that human sexuality is not an isolated article, as it is in the rest of the kingdom of the primates; it is a complex structure that starts and evolves in a sequence of erotogenic zones, combines those experiences of pleasure and pain in different styles, ending up as the distinct sexual preference of each individual subject.

There is no one particular endosomatic source for sexuality. Freud (1905d) said, "At its origin it [infantile sexual manifestations] attaches itself to one of the vital somatic functions; it has as yet no sexual object and is thus auto-erotic; its sexual aim is dominated by an erotogenic zone" (pp. 182–183).

The reason was one of Freud's unusual insights. He realized that the link between the endosomatic pressure and sexual pleasure are reversible[3]. So, although the sexual *Trieb* was supposed to represent the endosomatic source of stimulation, we discover that the endosomatic source, in turn, is also capable of representing the sexual *Trieb*. This insight answers the questions about the sexual nature of pleasures. If the two functions reciprocate in the process of representation, assigning different pleasures to each becomes irrelevant. But when Freud put all the pieces together, waiting for an intuition to set them ablaze, he faced a major problem: if sexuality is a *Trieb,* what is *Triebhaft* (instinctual) about it? In other words, if we put infantile sexuality, sexual perversion, the physical components of pleasure and the content-less *Trieb* all together it would be difficult to relate all that to the functions of sexuality as an urge, especially if we specify sexuality as an element of biological maturity that caters for the attraction between members of the opposite sexes, who seek genital union, originally, for procreation.

The Libido Theory: Problem or Solution

Although Freud used the term libido several times before the *Three Essays* (1905d) the clear and specific meaning it acquired in psychoanalysis came with the birth of the theory of infantile sexuality and remained so, especially when it became a constituent of the theory of *Trieb* and an important part of the

---

[3] Freud said (1905 b): "If, for instance, the common possession of the labial zone by two functions [sexuality and nourishment] is the reason why the sexual satisfaction arises during the taking of nourishment, then the same factor also enables us to understand why there should be disorders of the nutrition if the erotogenic functions of the common zone are disturbed. A good portion of the symptomatology of the psychoneuroses, which I have traced to the disturbances of the sexual processes is expressed in disturbances of other, nonsexual, somatic functions; and this circumstance, which has hitherto been unintelligible, becomes less puzzling if it is only the counterpart of the influences which bring about the production of sexual excitation" (205–206).

vocabulary of the new theories of psychopathology. The concept of the libido allowed sexuality to be framed within the concept of *Trieb,* but it became evident with time that it has shortcomings and inadequacies in dealing with the etiology of the psychoneuroses. The libido supported envisaging fixed causative relationship between sexual satisfaction-frustration and the psychoneurosis. Sexuality proved to be more complex than being an urge and what it was thought of as a need demanding satisfaction. However, Freud's insistence on keeping a place for sexuality in a theory of *Trieb* drove him to think of a solution to this dilemma. He thought of making the foundation of the viscidities of sexuality 'an energy.' Giving sexuality an energy that could express it, allowed him to talk about the transformations that are observed in infantile sexuality and in sexual deviations, the movement from one erotogenic zone to another, the plasticity to conform to the aims and objects of each zone. It also facilitated explaining the vicissitudes of the sexual phenomena without the need to explain separately the causation of each manifestation of sexuality. Nonetheless, Freud still had to find another *Trieb* that stands counter the sexual *Trieb* as its antithesis to remain capable of preserving the concept of psychodynamics. The antithesis of the sexual *Trieb* helped him to explain the known obstruction of sexual gratification, and to stay consistent with an expected natural duality in sexuality. An antithetical *Trieb* was indispensable in explaining the formation of symptoms in terms of conflict, which was at the time a dominant psychoanalytic paradigm.

Vital functions (physical demands) in the higher primates and humans are the same: they do not instigate separate pleasures associated with their gratification. The ambiguous difference between the vital functions and sexuality is the kind of energy behind the acts of gratifying their pressure. Vital urges subside when responded to pressure. There are no dualities in that regard. In sexuality, gratifying the urge does not totally end the urge, but just ends its pressure. Freud had to find a solution to the special duality in sexuality. He kept the term libido to mean the urge in sexuality. The energy invested in one's sexual issues he called *ego-libido.* In clarifying the matter, he said (1923b) "We thus reach the idea of quantity of libido, to the mental representation of which we give the name 'ego-libido,' and whose production, increase or diminution, distribution and displacement should afford us the possibility for explaining the psychosexual phenomena observed" (257). The distinction he made stipulated that libido in its original state is invested in the subject as an entity and not as separate functions. With time and maturation, a differentiation between the vital functions and their erotogenic zones happens and gets clearer. It was not clear, then, if what he meant by libido is a vital energy that branches out and differentiates later into sexual and vital energies, or there are two libidos that are practically fused at birth and differentiate later. He proceeded to call the vital functions with their libido 'ego-*Trieb*' and changed the name a little later to 'self-preservation *Trieb*' (1910k, pp. 213–216). It became confusing: were we on the verge of a new theory of the libido in which one libido would have two states based on where it was invested, or maybe we will do away with a separate theory of sexuality all together (1923b)?

However, he set the *ego-Trieb* as the antithesis of the *sexual Trieb* and set the two libidos to be in conflict because they differed in their *aims*: one aims to satisfy the vital needs, and the other aim is related to pleasure. He called the ego "the great reservoir of libido from which libido is sent to objects and which is always ready to absorb libido flowing from objects" (1923b, p. 257). The libido theory that came to solve the problem of what was *Triebhaft* in sexuality proved to be itself a problem. This discussion of sexuality, in terms of the libido theory, is merely of scholarly interest and value to the contemporary psychoanalyst. Nevertheless, we can see that even a straightforward function like sexuality is of dual nature in the human subject, whether we intend to underline it or not, *therefore we should keep in mind that the initiation of anything psychological does not happen outside a duality of sorts.*

The libido theory, although it was still relating strongly to sexuality, was no longer able to avoid its basic problem: *deciding* whether there is a separate sexual energy or sexuality is merely one of the manifestations of an energy that is not different from the quota of affect, which Freud used before to distinguish between affect and ideas (1894 a). Freud (1915c) said, "The concept of the quota of affect corresponds to the instinct in so far as the latter has become detached from the idea and finds expression, proportionate to its quantity, in processes which are sensed as affect" (p. 152). The libido theory was flawed because the content-less *Trieb* was transformed into a psychical function by a simple displacement of causes and effects. The libido, which is specifically related to pleasure, became an energy that looks for an object to invest in. Laplanche and Pontalis (1973) said, "The notion of 'ego-libido' does in fact entail a generalization of libidinal economy so as to embrace the whole of the interplay between cathexes and anticathexes, while whatever overtones of subjectivity the term 'libido' may have had hitherto are attenuated; as Freud acknowledges, the libido theory becomes frankly speculative" (p.240). The difficulties created by the libido theory, as a theory of energy, resulted in setting up series of awkward *dualities*: ego interests and a sexual *Trieb*, sexual *Trieb* and self-preservation *Trieb*, self-preservation *Trieb* and ego-*Trieb*, and ego-libido and object-libido. Finally, Freud settled on the duality of ego-libido and object-libido. This was the least challenging duality from a metapsychological point of view, but was theoretically more than challenging[6].

It meant that the libido – the core of a structural theory of sexuality – was an undefined energy and was identified only by where it was invested. Instead of the libido identifying its objects in the original theory, now it was identified by the objects it is invested in. The point of view that the subject's duality is not a result, an effect, or a means to explaining the uniqueness of the human attributes leads to a conclusion: *the subject's duality is the fundamental characteristic of his nature.*

Sexuality and the Wish

Freud's attention to the function of sexuality and its contribution to the formation of psychoneuroses were always seen in the context of causality. Even when he reversed the assertions about its role in psychopathology it maintained its quality as a factor in a process. However, his extensive exploration of sexuality and its origin in childhood revealed two characteristics that are seldom noticed or mentioned: 1. sexuality, in the human subject, goes through a process of development marked by distinctive phases. In each of those phases, sexuality undergoes changes that could be positive or negative and its development could even be arrested at any point of its progression, i.e., sex is not a 'thing' by virtue of its liability to fixate at any moment in its transformations. 2. Psychical life starts to show its animation when the fusion of the sexual function and the vital functions start to dissolve. Before that activation, both the vital and the sexual are stimulated by the same stimulus that emanates from the autoerotic zone. The development and maturation of those two functions separate them; the vital stimuli will remain straightforwardly biophysical, while the sexual will gain psychological significance and meaning and will be activated only by psychological stimuli. However, the response to those stimuli will be colored by the nature and the function of each zone. This is what was referred to (before) as the psychosexual basis of symptoms and personality, e.g., phallic personality or oral fanaticizing (Issacs, 1952). But we should keep in mind that the assumed original fusion of the sexual libido and the object will never be achieved completely. Psychoanalysts, who continue to adhere to the original discoveries about the subject, hear in the patient's speech and symptoms the echoes of the vital function within the sounds of the sexual functions. *We still can hear and notice how the subject's sexuality could tell us what we want to know about what to do and how to do it.* The working of the primary process is most evident in those moments when a sexual urge stimulates a vital wish which does the same reciprocally. This case is most present in alcohol addiction where the psychical dependency on alcohol is expressed in a metaphor of thirst.

The reason sexuality had its advantageous position in the discovery of psychoanalysis is to be found in the nature of its duality. Seeking pleasure and avoiding pain is one of the basic principles of life. The vital functions could be a source of pain if not responded to, e.g., the pain of hunger, but also a source of pleasure if the subject becomes aware of the subsiding pain. At the beginning (birth), the vital needs and pleasure are fused in one combined act – the act of sucking the breast. But their fusion is destined to dissipate with time because of the subject's natural duality of the active *I* and the observing *I* will be able to deal separately with satisfying a vital need and the disappearance of pain. Better, the likely separations of the act of ending pain from experiencing pleasure creates a sense of a process, i.e., consciousness of the duality of the object and the aim of the *Trieb*. The newly born would eventually form an idea (fantasy) about his oral object and connect it with the act of sucking. The fusion of the vital and the sexual in orality is destined to dissipate when the duality of the infant-subject apperceives the feeding situation.

It is not difficult for clinical psychoanalysts to envisage the variety of experiences the infant goes through and apperceives him in the oral phase. The outcome will decide the way mouth and breast will become organs of pleasure. The reason is that the same will happen in the next psychosocial phase of development; the anal phase. The outcome of that phase will join and add to the system of pleasure. The subject's sexuality, which is supposed to be dominated by the erotogenesis of the genital zone, will be decided by those experiences. Sexuality in humans is the meeting point of several fundamentals in the psychical life of the subject.

To sum up we can say that almost all the wishes the subject will experience later in life are dealt with within the process of sexual maturation. This is why the subject's character decides his sexuality and not the other way around. Sex is the mother of all wishes because all wishes have to get their particular significance from the way they were dealt with during sexual maturation. *Sex is not a wish it is the prototype of wishing*

Chapter Seven
The Duality of Life and Death
A Basis for Narcissism

There are discoveries in the theory of psychoanalysis which were considered by some unrelated to the rest of the clinical findings or the basic theory. Yet, with some attention and 'keeping' the faith we discover later their correctness and significance. Every discovery about the human subject has a natural basic nature that makes it relate to the other discoveries in a natural way, though sometimes unexpectedly. One of those discoveries is the notion of life and death in the psychoanalytic theory. Most of the glorification of this duality at the time Freud brought it to attention (1920g) came mostly from a blind faith that Freud must have landed a new discovery, which will be a turning point in psychoanalysis. But it was soon neglected, and even some rejected it decidedly. My view is that it is a concept which explains another equally confusing concept that could not find a place in psychoanalysis out of the libido theory, i.e. narcissism. Therefore, mentioning aspects of the libido theory that link narcissism to the death instinct could be of clinical value after all.

The duality of ego libido and sexual libido (see last chapter) led Freud to an unexpected configuration of the duality of the human subject as a whole, which the scholars of psychoanalysis call a turning point (1920g). Discussing the libido theory at that stage of the evolution of psychoanalysis, particularly in its clinical aspect, would seem – and actually is – far from being of interest or use to psychoanalysts. Nevertheless, concepts like psychical energy, degree of intensity, pressure, attachment and detachment, advancement and regression, were still part and parcel of talking about psychological phenomena in any of the known clinical trends then and in the current schools of psychoanalysis. Strangely, the concept of libido provides an easy useful conception that adjusts to any of the phenomena highlighted in those schools, and has the advantage of being part of the original theory that all contemporary theories branched out from, though most of them just deny. Thus, the 'libido' could still give the impression that we are all still the same psychoanalysts.

I do not mean that we should go back to the libido theory as part of our theoretical heritage.

As mentioned in the last chapter, Freud reversed the cause-effect relationship in the etiology of psychoneuroses by which sexuality was not the latent cause of the neurosis but neurosis was active in changing the sexuality of the subject. In hindsight, we could say that *Freud needed a concept that is able to turn sexuality into a 'result' of something instead of being the cause of things*. However, when Freud took a new angle in dealing with sexuality based on its infantile roots, he realized that he had to explore and deal with the different objects of libidinal investment. Getting attached to objects libidinally – like the ego and the non-ego – affects the kind of modification that has to happen to the libido to achieve that. Libidinal attachment to the mother changes from attachment to the breast to attachment to the mother as whole. This new Freudian development looked then as a significant change in the concept of libido, but it was more subtle than significant. The libido was originally the specific energy of both the desire and the act of sexual intercourse but in its new conception it is energy with the specific quality of malleability that allows it to get invested in different sexual aims and objects; but still in a sexual connotation[1].

Recognizing infantile sexuality and its devolvement toward sexual maturity proved that the libido is better considered in quantitative terms. Yet its terminology allows qualitative descriptions of psychoanalytic issues in general, like weakness and strength and latency and activity, etc. It also facilitates dealing with the flexibility of the sexual urge in its course of development, which depended on changes in its intensity according to the demand of the aims and the objects of each stage of development. Although the libido was the *term* used by most in dealing with sexual activities, it gradually became a concept in its own right and became independent of its sexual connotation. It proved to be a practical vocabulary to describe all matters that have fixed definitions but undergo changes in intensities.

Narcissism is a good example of the usefulness of the term libido in psychoanalysis. The libido also proved that we could talk about the normal and abnormal phenomena with the same vocabulary. Point in fact; sexuality

---

[1] Freud's psychoanalysis – in real terms – is the whole process of insights and intuitions along with the revisions of those aspects. The half century between the concept of repression and of mental representation has the history of psychoanalysis within it; not just the 'landmarks' on the way from point to point. A theory of the subject has to come out of Freud's interconnected phases of psychoanalysis.

necessitated the creation of the concept of psychical energy or libido, but once it was created it proved to be able to put several psychoanalytic observations in a more common and understandable language. The libido was intended to explain sexuality but it ended up being an entity that is explained by sexuality (or the principle of pleasure-pain).

Moreover, its flexibility suggested a solution to two problems. First, what is the state of the libido before it divides and engenders the several dualities mentioned above? Second, is the divided libido a separation in a single urge or a division to separate urges that should have their own duos? I will deal later with the clinical implications of answering those questions and the risk of practicing psychoanalysis without clarification of those points.

The first characteristic regarding the libido, whether it is one or two, is that it is there from the moment of birth. There is nothing physically known that could have had the power to create the libido after birth. Thus, the original libido must have been there before determining its duality or singularity.

The subject is born with his libidinal charge, which should eventually be behind both the vital functions and the psychological leanings. So, if we have one libido it will originally and normally be invested in the subject, and gradually let parts of it to be invest in objects[2]. If we have two libidos which are fused at birth, the parts that are destined to be object-libido will gradually withdraw from the subject and get invested in his objects[3]. As a malleable energy it could move from an object to another as it could also take the subject as an object creating what was mentioned above as 'narcissism.' This is a significant point in the argument, because whether we have one libido or two *the subject will always have a narcissistic component to his being emanating from the onset of libidinal investments.*

---

[2] Contemporary psychoanalysts would find this classical terminology strange and impractical. However, this terminology and the concepts behind them were the means that created psychoanalysis, i.e., talked about specific matters that put the subject in his own perspective, and were unavailable to any other mode of thinking about the subject. They were and still are the way we should consider, if we agree that the subject matter of psychoanalysis is the subject.

[3] Freud introduced the concept of narcissism saying (1914c): "I should like at this point [arguing the separation between the two libidos, ego and sexual] expressly to admit that hypothesis of separate ego-instinct and sexual instincts (that is to say, the libido theory) rests scarcely at all upon a psychological basis but derives its principal support from biology. But I shall be consistent enough [with my general rule] to drop this hypothesis if psychoanalytic work should itself produce some other, more noticeable hypothesis about instincts" (79).

The natural state of affairs of the libido is being invested in the subject first as its starting point; then gets invested in his objects. Therefore, clinically speaking, it is *not* correct to expect normality in the subject whose basic and starting nature is narcissistic. Narcissism has always been considered a pathological condition and a diagnostic category. This limited understanding of narcissism comes from the libido theory itself. When the libido is partially invested in the subject – who is its original base – and resists leaving its base or withdraws from it to be reinvested in that base. Clinicians called that narcissistic disorder. As we will see a little later, narcissism has very little to do with libidinal investment and is more an issue relating to the identity of the subject. The simple change of the term from 'sexual-libido' or 'ego-libido' to 'narcissistic-libido' (1920g) should not have changed anything significant in the theory. Yet, it introduced a very noteworthy clarification of the previous insights regarding the erotogenic phases of development, the birth of the concepts of fixation and repetition compulsion in psychopathology, and the dynamics of therapy and cure (transference). In every phase of development, there is a stage where the libido has to go through the specific narcissism of that stage, as a step before going any further to the next stage, i.e., the libido does not move from the object of an erotogenic zone to the object of the next zone. It moves from the subject of the phase to its object. For the infant to move from the oral stage to the anal stage he has to relate narcissistically to the breast to free his libido to go further to the next phase. This innocuous introduction of a narcissistic stage in every developmental stage (Freud, 1914c) changed Freud's theory in a radical way. Freud was no longer able to rely on the mechanical model of 'an ego defending itself' or a psyche that is a product of the success or the failure of strengthening the ego. It was clear that the ego was no longer a particular agent of the individual but had to be either the whole person or none of the individual. If the ego is the reservoir of the libido then it must have existed before the libido ever existed. *It makes more sense to say that the ego is a product of narcissism than to assume the existence of the ego prior to any other psychical events, phenomena, or system.* Moreover, Freud said (1914 c): "I may point out that we are bound to suppose that a unity comparable to the ego cannot exist in the individual from the start; the ego has to be developed. The autoerotic instincts, however, are there from the very first; so, there must be something added to autoerotism – a new psychical action – in order to bring about narcissism" (p. 76). The importance of that statement and its discussion proves that Freud was thinking clinically about the problem. Although he did not use narcissism properly to solve problems of dualities in the libido theory, it is clear that he could not have proceeded without paying attention to the narcissistic nature of the subject's

103

dualities. Laplanche and Pontalis (1973) said, "If we preserve a distinction between a state on the one hand in which the sexual instincts attain satisfaction anarchically, independently of one another, and narcissism on the other hand, where the ego in its entirety is taken as a love-object, then we must inevitably make a period of infantile narcissism's dominance coincide with the formative moment of the ego" (p. 256). A careful clinician needs to know if he is interpreting an issue or the narcissistic copy of that issue.

Life and Death of Trieben and Narcissism

Six years after the introduction of narcissism to the theory of psychoanalysis Freud published a puzzling work: *Beyond the Pleasure Principle* (1920g). It introduced a new *Triebhaft,* a duality of life and death to replace the previous duality of sex and self-preservation. There were two obvious and declared reasons for that shift, one theoretical (to understand the phenomena of aggression, sadism, masochism, hate, and ambivalence), and another one of clinical root which accounts for the phenomenon of repetition compulsion. The theoretical reason was conspicuously weak. Those phenomena did not constitute any theoretical problem and were quite explainable in terms of the other *Triebhaft* dualities. Besides, they did not get substantially clearer in the new theory of life/death. However, Freud raised some important issues about *primary* sadism and masochism, suggesting that there might be latent conditions in human nature waiting for occasions to sprout contents and express themselves. This suggestion was far-fetched but plausible in light of the theory of *Trieb* and his old concept of bound and unbound states of excitation (1894a).

The clinical phenomenon of repetition compulsion is worth careful scrutiny because it was not a new clinical discovery, yet it was about to take a new meaning in the life and death *Trieben*. Previously, it was dealt with under the concept of *fixation* without much fuss. However, it looks as if Freud suddenly made a distinction between fixation and the compulsion to repeat, and it came only after the introduction of the concept of narcissism. Therefore, we have to question the link between the significance Freud gave to the compulsion to repeat after highlighting the phenomenon of narcissism. The significance of the compulsion to repeat is not related, in any major way, to introducing the new *Triebhaft* duality of life and death, which was considered by many analysts 'a turning point' in a theory of drives. Yet, repetition compulsion was intriguing by itself because it redirected us to what was left behind in the theory of dreams and the theory of *Trieb*. The wish, like the *Trieb*, uses the same mechanisms of the primary process in expressing themselves.

However, Freud did not explain how the wish and the *Trieb* go about acquiring contents to express themselves and become psychological entities. This point passed unnoticed but the concept of narcissism put it forcefully in the heart of the theory of psychoanalysis.

On the one hand, the first theory of *Trieb* captured a duality between the power of pleasure (sexuality) and the strength of restriction (ego). On the other hand, it presented a dynamic interplay between the preservation of the species (sex) and the preservation of the individual (self-preservation). The problems mentioned above regarding this model could boil down to a functional duality that had neither a structural foundation nor leads to a structural duality. It seems that narcissism (in libidinal terms) put Freud face-to-face with a basic issue: the existence of something *primal* preparing for a sequel to form. The sequel is the secondary form of the primary state (primary narcissism engenders secondary narcissism). The emergence of consciousness from unconsciousness leads to a parallel of the emergence of life, particularly psychological life, from 'pre-psychical-life.' His heuristic explorations in 'Beyond the Pleasure Principle' have the characteristics of a search for something that should be there to explain something that has been discovered but is waiting to be defined. (Fayek, 2009)

Freud, intuitively, considered life and death as the bedrock of human dualities that explains the most basic phenomenon in human nature: *the ongoing state of becoming, evolving, and dying.* Although this might sound presumptuous, speculative, and not psychoanalytic, it is actually an elaboration of Freud's insight about a life and death *Trieben* as the instincts 'par-excellence.' All *Trieben* in psychoanalysis have a teleological undertone of progress and change, while instincts in the rest of the animal kingdom do not seem to have more than the propensity to routinely repeat the past.

Narcissism stands at the crossroads of the life and death *Trieben*. Life *Trieb* is expressed in love, preservation of self, attraction, the inclination to unite, and the pleasure of relating. Those attributes are narcissistic even in the popular simplistic conception of the word of 'selfishness.' Yet, narcissism – at the same time – is the source of hating what interferes with self-interest and explains the preference to withdraw into the self. Selfishness in relating to others depicts lifeless relationships. It is in the psychical state where we encounter ambivalence and the emergence of *Triebhaft* contradictory tendencies. Narcissism presents potential dualities that needed to be structuralized. A life *Trieb* is easier to accept if only because it denotes some things that we know and live with. The problem with the death *Trieb* starts with the name. It is supposed to denote, in psychoanalysis, 'what is before life and what is after it.' It is also difficult to *distinguish* the psychical representations of the death

Trieb, although it generated over the centuries an abundance of symbolic forms of itself. Moreover, defining it in terms of the four elements of the *Trieb*: *source, pressure, aim,* and *object* is only possible by speculation, if at all. Practically, there are no synonyms which could specify different attribute to the finality of death.

The concept has created a great deal of argument, and most analysts have relinquished it for various expressed reasons, mostly related to its clinical irrelevance. Nonetheless, we cannot do away with the concept of the death *Trieb* without doing away with concept of narcissism, which we should not do. We should find a way to keep the baby even if we have to throw out the bathwater. The historical connection between the two concepts in Freud's text is difficult to ignore, and the link has forced major revisions of the early theoretical formulations, like metapsychology and anxiety. We still cannot find in Freud's work a psychological equivalent that connects the death *Trieb* to a purely biological evidence of death, or something related to practice, whatever that might be. Yet, Freud must have found something in the myth of narcissus to name this psychological condition, as he did with the Oedipus complex[4]. The choice of the myth of Narcissus to describe a libidinal state is incomprehensible without looking at its content and structure together, not only separately. Narcissus is a myth that begins with a question about death and life, and ends with a question regarding life and death. In an exercise in psychoanalytic thinking, we could 'tentatively' work from the myth toward psychoanalysis, with the anticipation that if we could do that correctly we could reverse this process later to work backward from psychoanalysis to the myth, and still reach the same results.

A Brief Account of the Myth Goes Like This

When Narcissus was born, his mother, Liriope, asked Teiresias the seer whether her newborn child will live a long life. He replied, "*If he never knew himself.*" Narcissus grew up to be a very beautiful youth who was adored by many suitors of both sexes. Among those who loved him in vain was the nymph 'Echo.' She had previously been doomed by the goddess Hera to repeat the last words spoken to her. Hence, Echo was unable to initiate a conversation with Narcissus and her love for him was incommunicable. Her speech was

---

[4] Freud's choice of the Oedipus myth to describe the interfamilial tensions and dynamics is easy to appreciate and fathom. It is the core of Freud's discovery of the part parental roleplays in structuring the intrapsychic.

wasted in just 'echoing' him. As a result, he did not recognize her and she vanished within his own voice.

A young man, whom Narcissus had spurned, as he spurned many others, put a curse on him to love unrequitedly. Nemesis, the goddess of retribution, arranged it so that Narcissus would see his reflection on the surface of a pond. He fell in love with his image, not knowing that it is his reflection, and laid down beside the water neither able to attract the attention of whoever was in the pond nor able to tear himself away from the reflection of his image. He faded away and was transformed into a flower beside the water. This is where he lives now and forever after 'knowing' himself as the seer said.

Echo died as a subject that had a silent counterpart, while Narcissus died waiting for a subject who was in the pond and who could not become his counterpart to reciprocate the admiration. Teiresias's prophecy was thus fulfilled; Narcissus knew himself and died loving it (Tripp, 1970).

Lévi-Strauss (1955) said, "A myth always refers to events alleged to have taken place long ago. But what gives a myth an operational value is the specific pattern described is timeless; it explains the present and the past as well as the future" (p. 209).

The underlying theme of the myth of Narcissus is the theme of actualized and materialized existence that is born dead before its actual death. Echo was *present* but faded away into narcissus's voice; she was another but could not be to Narcissus the needed another. Echo died because she could not become alive and Narcissus's counterpart. Her death is the symbolic death of the counterpart that emerges from Narcissism (one's self). Narcissus withered away into feeling nothing for anyone but his-self when he encountered 'himself.' He left behind a flower that represented his silent patience. The value of the myth is instituted in its structure as a metaphor; Narcissism is *psychological death*.

The structural theme of the myth is the symbolic absence in a presence and the false presence in an absence. Echo was present but because of her impediment she was absent. Narcissus was absent in his reflection on the water, though he was present in front of that absence. The narcissistic person has a silent *I* in himself that has nothing genuine to say. He talks *for* something that is absent. He is a person without a desire to articulate but waits for the other – the counterpart – to give him an object for his content-less wishes. Being a creation awaiting to be born, he waits for the other to reflect to him his-self to know it, while the other is just a mirror reflecting to him his image. The narcissist's desire will be either what the other articulates or – as sometimes happens – the opposite of what the other articulates as the ultimate range of freedom the narcissist could reach. The narcissistic person is psychologically not alive. Grunberger (1979) argued that narcissism could be a defense against the death *Trieb* saying: "One question comes to mind is whether the subjective value of the Eros-Thanatos hypothesis does not lie in the fact that it serves as a shield against the narcissistic wound of death as organic deterioration (arousing the fear of disintegration), an implacable process that sneaks up on us and to which each of us must succumb" (p. 241).

Narcissistic attachments are characterized by a sense of absence of something in every attachment. The reason we are not finding the psychological equivalent of the death *Trieb* in our practice comes from Freud's conception of the ego, which could still captivate us as it did to psychoanalysts for a long time. As mentioned above, Freud's conception of the subject is of an ontological entity that has an unqualified existence, i.e., an existence that has no cause or explanation, but awaits a cause to explain its existence. It was impossible for Freud to have considered the *I* as the whole subject. He was constantly looking for 'what' could explain the psychical phenomena without the need for finding its causation. This made him try, many times, to bring matters to a wrap-up, but his will to have a true theory of psychoanalysis stopped him every time from self-deception. Therefore, he could not ignore that the *I* is in a tie with a counterpart of the speaking person (*me*). He could not miss that the duality of *I-me* relationship is exactly the situation narcissus has created in front of his image.

Freud stated in his paper on Negation (1925 h) that the ego, sometimes, instead of repressing something it just denies it, For instance, saying "I did not mean to offend you" is admitting the notion of offending but negating it as if it was not there in the first place. In fact, the *I* (ego) does not negate or denies; it expresses what is in the sphere of the *Ucs.*, and denies its existence in the sphere of the *Cs*. Therefore, we should consider the ego a function of the counterpart and not its adversary. Narcissus sought after a counterpart but that counterpart he found was he himself, which made him what he was: the person who is merely an *I* that is falsely used as the true *me*. *Narcissism is caught between the subjective I and a false objective me, not between the ego and the other.* Narcissism is an issue in the subject's persistent inclination to define his identity because he is not able to define his reflection as his image and not his-self.

Clinically, we frequently encounter the patient who suffers and complains of loneliness because he is not liked by people for no reason he knows. He always finds himself with the wrong others who refrain from getting close to him. That patient is not caught in wrong relationships but is captivated by a relationship between him and his dislikeable self-image.

108

Understanding narcissism this way allows understanding the problem of the counterpart that eluded Western culture until Freud came. He discovered that the dream is the speech of the counterpart and was also able to decipher the language of the dream-work. He discovered that in waking life, the counterpart still speaks the same language he uses when the subject is asleep but it requires a different code of interpretation to translate. In sleep, there is only the *me* listening, while in waking life both the *I* and the *me* are talking and listening at the same dream, sometimes in harmony and sometimes in conflict, but mixing the particulars of the primary process and the characteristics of the secondary process.

Back to Psychoanalysis

The Cartesian Cogito initiated the philosophical enterprise of discovering the nature of the 'subject.' The philosophical work came to underline and explicate the feature of duality in the subject, which is the very central human feature. The duality of the subject permeates his psychical life as well as his cognitive tendencies. However, when philosophy reached that point in its theory of the subject it came to crossing the gap that exists in every duo in the subject's dualities. The reason is that the dualities look as if they are the making of the subject, yet the subject is never aware of the process of making him make them. Psychoanalysis came with the solution when Freud noted the splitting of consciousness and the birth of the unconscious. The Freudian *unconsciousness proved to be a process and not a psychical condition or entity. The unconscious is the process that transforms what is potentially conscious into material that is foreign to the secondary process.* Thus, psychoanalysis embarked on a major endeavor that gradually made the subject a subject for discoveries, that are still in action and needed to continue.

The foundation on those discoveries is the concept of unconsciousness. The difficulty in dealing with unconsciousness is the tendency to forget that it is a psychical process and not a psychological state. This means that no external effort or clarification could initiate any change in it, and a change has to come from modifying the process that creates it. For instance, if during the work of analysis, the patient shows (not reveals) features of narcissistic injury, no talking or explanations of that handicapping condition would change anything about it. Interpreting the material that expresses such injury as a specific response to an event or the misunderstanding of situations could change the unconscious process of compulsive repetition and the power of repetition weakens because in the process of unconscious, the hurt is revealed. As a process it could be changed if something from within the process is changed. Examining this difference has important benefits both clinically and theoretically. Clinically, we have to tune in to the way the *I* and the *me* are dynamically creating the situations, including the analytic situation and the dialogue with the analyst. There is a significant difference between dealing with the action of the *I* or the *me* as separate agents in the formation of a transference response or as a duality that does not differentiate between them in the analytic situation.

A clinical vignette could clarify this issue:

A young woman came out of a serious situation that caused her deep depression, and almost made her lose a good inheritance. Her daily life changed – in a short period of time – to scenes of exhibitionism and acting silly but did not reach the quality or level of hypomania. After few months of that change she expressed her discomfort with the change. She said that she is constantly looking for means and ways to feel important, and that is making her tense all the time. After few more associations, she put it this way: "I look for ways to make people make me feel important." I underlined to her that she did not notice (unconsciously) that she does not feel important and needs people to do something for her about it. Few sessions went in expanding and elaborating the link between what she wanted and what she gets. Then came an insight: when she was a child, she had a brother who was four years older. He died few years early in their childhood of a blood condition. Her mother's grief and her father's sadness left her with the impression that she was living a fantasy of importance, while her brother was really the only important member of the family.

Clinically, this memory was a joint insight that the exaltation she reported in the previous sessions was not about a psychological state of 'exaltation.' It was an unconscious way to indirectly recall her childhood disappointment: *I* am not important, but I will make people make *me* important (unconscious narcissistic deprivation). The childhood narcissistic hurt made her affected *I* become – metaphorically – her Echo, and metonymically her psychically dead Narcissus. The patient died psychologically with abolishing her sense of importance in childhood and lived and relived her narcissistic death every morning when she awaked to do what could bring her confirmation of importance.

Theoretically, knowing how to listen to the patient in both his capacity as an *I* and a *me,* or in his particular narcissistic structure, makes the analyst pay more attention to the process of interpretation: what is interpreting, what to interpret, and to whom he should direct the interpretation. The analyst has to be clear about what to interpret: the patient's narrative, or the implicit appeal to the analyst to understand. It is also important to know what words to use in interpreting, because interpretations become part of the next material the patient will come up with. When I chose to say 'did not notice' I wanted to keep the vocabulary within the cognitive functions to avoid distractions in the intricacies of the unconscious (was too early for that).

Keeping the interpretation within the interpersonal relations between the patient and the people he deals with or the 'others' was also necessary at that stage. Later in the analysis the intrapsychic dynamics became the core of the psychotherapeutic interpretative process. Nothing I could have done, as an analyst, to change the unconscious effects of her childhood insight about her and her brother. Words and explanations would have been empty wards. But when that insight was linked in a smooth and non-pretentious way to her present living experience the work of interpretation and reconstruction was possible. She was then in a lived transference relationship with the analysts that could get meaning and be assimilated in the structure of the transference. Interpretations could produce some structural changes to the patient's self-image: the authentic *I*. Literarily, psychoanalyzing should be done when the patient is ready to become alive in the manifestation of transference. Interpretation of transference brings the psychologically dead patient to life. *Acquiring the sense of what is said in the patient's association, what to interpret and when and how, comes from knowing well what the subject is, not what psychoanalysis is. Knowing the subject is the learning part in the training in psychoanalysis.*

Addendum

Most the psychoanalytic discoveries are interconnected either by the links of their evolution or by their input in a main psychical structure. This is natural in a theory about the same phenomenon: the human subject. The phenomenon of after-effect links with the return of the repressed, and the topographic point of view suggested the dynamic point of view. However, two important discoveries in the theory seem to have weak linkage with the rest of the discoveries and barely have any relation between them: narcissism and the death instinct.

Narcissism in the libido theory is a condition that could have a biological connotation stemming from the withdrawal of the libido from the objects or the external world and investing it in the subject instead. This psychological condition could be the biological equivalent of a state of death, i.e., the biological equivalent of narcissism is psychical death. At the same time Freud said (1920 g) that the most valuable missing part of the theory is a psychological distinction between ego libido and sexual libido (ibid). Thus, the psychological equivalent of repetition compulsion is also psychical. Unintentionally and very subtly Freud linked the two ambiguous concepts theoretically through the death *Trieb* by raising the issues of the duality of the libido and the duality of the pleasure principle and the compulsion to repeat. Underling this characteristic in the theory of psychoanalysis is meant to show that psychoanalysis is a theory of the subject.

We can surmise from the connection he made between the two separate but parallel lines of thinking in the theory that there is a link of sorts between the biological and the psychological factors in narcissism and the compulsion to repeat. Since that link was not formulated by Freud, I will venture and try my understanding of the issue. The parallelism between narcissism and the death instinct indicates the arrest of a natural process of development that is supposed to free the biological from the psychological and allowing the subject to reach his potentials. The clinical feature of this process is expressed in the adult patient who still relates to love to feeding and intimacy to touching and 'experiences' the psychological and the biological as interchangeable.

Chapter Eight
The Subject and the Unconscious
The Aconscious

The discovery of the unconscious was a gradual process, and Freud gave it several meanings along the way. He was not definite about its connotation, and oscillated between functional meanings like 'the repressed' and the result of the splitting of consciousness, and structural meanings like the systemic unconscious and the non-repressed unconscious. The problem with the unconscious is its participating in the creation of all of psychical phenomena, but in varied ways, which requires different adjectives to correspond to its contribution to those phenomena.

The unconscious is initially a French discovery. When Charcot in Paris, and both Liébeault and Bernhiem in Nancy used hypnosis to examine splitting of consciousness in hysteria, Freud got interested and brought their ideas and techniques back to Vienna. His work with Breuer, and continuing on his own, paved the way to identify unconsciousness as a separate psychical entity, and not an event or product of other psychical events. Not long after that conclusion he worked on discovering psychoanalysis as a theory of 'something!' He is the adoptive father of the French endeavor, but also the actual and legitimate father of the 'unconscious' that is acknowledged now as the core of psychoanalysis.

When he started with psychoanalysis, the unconscious was an *object* (undesirable things, i.e., psychical material that is severed from consciousness), then, he realized the unconscious as a subjective process and a phenomenon of each individual patient. The unconscious changed from being things banished from consciousness to a factual production of the psychical life of the *subject.*

His work with patients widened his understanding of the nature of what is in splitting of consciousness, and what becomes unconscious of it and how. The process of splitting of consciousness was no longer enough to explain the experience of unconsciousness. Thus, he gave that process the *adjective* of a process that could make psychical subjects and objects split from consciousness and rendered unconscious. In spite of his long and serious endeavors to get to the core of this especial process, and his success in reaching that core, he could not see the full extent and the perspective of the adjectival nature of 'unconsciousness.' He remained – forcibly – loyal to the functional understanding of psychical phenomena. It is our responsibility to unfold Freud's discovery of the unconscious and give it its structural meaning. The unconscious turns out to be the spinal column of any theory of psychoanalytic nature. Yet, it was, and still is, the most confusing and unsettled concept in the classical theory, and strangely has little presence in the contemporary schools[1] of psychoanalysis. The unconscious in the literature of those schools is hardly mentioned as a factor in either psychopathology or psychotherapy.

Freud left the concept in an unsettled state, but not intentionally. This is obvious in his last metapsychology: the structural theory. The structural theory seemed to be reasonably comprehensive but it had no place for the unconscious in it. Freud had to go back to the topographic metapsychology to find it a place in what was supposedly his last and complete metapsychology. Doing that necessitated giving the ego a slice of unconsciousness leading to discovering a new unconscious; *the non-repressed unconscious* (Freud, 1923 b). Over the years, several forms and changes happened to that concept. However, in whatever meaning the unconscious was used it was and still is the most central in any possible theory of the subject. The reason is that is the permeation of unconscious characteristics in all human phenomena regardless of the theory the thinker is using.

The Cartesian duality led us to narcissism as the primary link between the active and the observing *I*. Yet, the relationship between the duos in that duality contains few unsettled ideas: are they conscious of each other? If not, could one be conscious of the other? If so, which one would it be? If one is unconscious what function does the unconscious achieves in that duality? If we go back to chapter two and the philosophers' impasse regarding the dualities of the subject, we will notice that the difficulties they encountered were due to the silent existence of those three questions which remained without answers in their philosophical conceptions. If psychoanalysis came up with the solution to the philosophical impasse it was because it provided a

---

[1] There is no agreed upon enumeration of the schools of psychoanalysis because there is no agreement on what to consider a school and what is not. However, I could mention a number of titles to give some idea about what is regarded a school: The cathartic theory, the structural theory, ego psychology, object relations theory, self-psychology, interpersonal psychoanalyses, intersubjective theory.

promising perspective of consciousness and unconsciousness that could deal with those three questions.

The most central in Freud's discovery of unconsciousness is an idea that merits more attention. Unconsciousness is a function of two independent systems. There is unconsciousness of material that was conscious at a time and then was unconscioused[2] (this is what is usually called repression). There is also unconsciousness of material that were never conscious at any point before (better to call it a-conscious)[3]. The majority of the psychoanalysts used both types of the unconscious as one and the same, without noticing that this fusion gives the unconscious the meaning it has in psychology. The psychological meaning of the unconscious is what does not exist in a conscious state, i.e., a cognitive understanding of consciousness. The cognitive unconscious is material that was once present in consciousness but barred from it by repression, yet could in principle be retrieved. Freud called that kind preconscious *Pcs.*, because its martial is merely latent. The second meaning of unconsciousness or the 'a-conscious' is material that never existed before in the sphere of cognition; therefore, they remain irretrievable (like preverbal psychical experiences).

He later named that material systemic unconscious and referred to that with the abbreviation *Ucs.* (1915 e). The distinction he made between the *Ucs.* and the *Pcs.* is important to note for two reasons: (a) The *Ucs.* processes are inadmissible to consciousness not because of their content (function), but because of their nature (structure). They do not lend themselves to the rules of the secondary process and get representations; they stay in their primitive states. The processes that form a dream are interactions between the day's residue (*Pcs.*) and infantile events that are totally unconscious (*Ucs.*). The process that keeps a piece of consciousness systemically unconscious is Freud's contribution to the theory of the subject. This point shows that the

---

[2] Freud used this passive form of negation to suggest that sometimes consciousness does not provide (does not have) neither complete nor trustworthy knowledge of certain processes. He used the term unconscioused in the 'project' (1950 a, p.308) to specifically distinguish that state from repression proper.

[3] The prefix 'un,' when added to adjectives, nouns, or adverbs carries the meaning of 'not.' Un-consciousness is the familiar theory of the unconscious in psychoanalysis. However, as I will explain later, psychoanalysis has another concept of the unconsciousness of psychical material that have no means to become conscious, although they are not repressed. I chose to use the prefix 'a' to mean without, as in amorphous, asexual, atypical, etc.

unconscious is not a psychical entity but an active process that conflicts with consciousness all the time.

His new insight regarding 'dream work' revoked the notion that repression is what creates unconsciousness. It is the workings of the primary process that changes the nature of the psychical material into material that is adjectivally unconscious. The ambitions, animosities, grandiosity, and the rest of Freud's intrapsychic life – in the *Irma* dream – were expressed but in a different language than the conscious language. Dream interpretation revealed that they were not only accomplished but they had 'what I feel or think' about the situation. In his statement mentioned above (1900a, p.62) he emphasized that the origin and structure of the psychical material and not its nature is what makes the difference. This distinction gives us two meanings of unconsciousness: an adjectival meaning which fits the preconscious, and a substantive meaning which describes the first type (Laplanche &Pontalis, 1973).

Freud combined the conscious and the preconscious in one system that contrasts with the unconscious as system. The reason to combine the *Pcs.* and *Cs.* in one and the same system is the dynamic relationship between the two systems, and the relative ease by which psychical material could move from one to the other. But the most important difference is the nature of the relation of the signified to the signifier. Both the conscious and the preconscious are products of the secondary processes; therefore, their content could be explained in the same way and the same language. Freud's conscious concern (the *Irma Dream*) about making a mistake in the diagnosis is the same in its nature as his ideas of grandiosity: he could 'talk' about both consciously using the same expressive modes.

The aconscious (*Ucs.*) is not admissible to consciousness or retrievable because its material has only one means to do that: creating a representation of itself to send first to the system *Pcs.\Cs.* Therefore, the *Ucs.* could only be revealed but when the representation is 'interpreted.' Interpretation turns the unconscious conscious by changing the quality of the content into secondary process material. For instance, an aconscious sense of deprivation could send to consciousness a sense of 'emptiness' (remainder of oral experiences), yet still misses the feature of consciousness. The second representation of a sense of general dissatisfaction and fulfillment is what stays in consciousness as the context of conscious experiences. In order for something to gain access to consciousness, it has to acquire a qualitative form and a subjective relevance (qualia) that could be turned into the process of cognitive expression.

Freud's dealing with the *Ucs.* showed that the aconscious is capable of being transformed into *Pcs.* material by getting attracted to other endeavors.

Those endeavors are – in themselves – already part of the functions of consciousness. An adolescent patient developed compulsive pulling of her hair (absent-mindedly). She was diagnosed as alopecia-areata. Talking about her childhood she precociously delved into the family situation and her mother's unreasonable expectations and demands. She also revealed a preconscious old grudge against her mother because of the different expectation she had of her and her other sister. The patient harbored childhood rage at an unreasonable mother, but was not even preconscious of it later. When the analyst commented (you wanted to pull your hair every time your mother got into one of her fits) the young woman could not stop laughing and crying the rest of the interview. The symptom represented the aconscious childhood problem with rage. The rage remained aconscious until adolescence. In doing so the patient revealed that the aconscious employed the rules of the primary process and represented the affective state of despair in the non-verbal actual pulling of her hair. The fleeting interpretation turned the symptom into a secondary process that would allow 'talking about the childhood experiences' that were 'represented' in pulling hair. Interpreting the representation of aconscious material (sense of emptiness) could reveal the links with a precocious wish to have more, or feeling that what is available is not enough. If that becomes part of free association the analyst could then give the aconscious venues to link with earlier experiences. Point in fact, in any advanced analysis it is difficult to find analytic material that is not of that nature. Experience shows that missing that angle in analytic work turns it into an endlessness process.

Psychoanalyzing is the act of revealing the unconscious process that transformed a childhood meaning into conscious adult issue, and giving the patient the chance to own that transformation, so he can change it if he so wished.

The Puzzling Unconscious

Laplanche and Pontalis said (1973): "If Freud's discovery had to be summed up in a single word, that word would without any doubt have to be 'unconscious'" (p. 474). This sweeping statement is not a frivolous subjective consideration of psychoanalysis. Freud's other discoveries and ideas are only meaningful, internally connected, and show consistency despite the several modifications they went through, because the unconscious permeates them all because it is fundamental and has evident presence in the fabric of psychological life. It is more accurate to say that the discovery of psychoanalysis is a result of discovering the unconscious, than to say that the unconscious is the most important discovery in psychoanalysis. It is also evident that the *Ucs.* 's substantive meaning, as the distinction made by Freud in the topographical model of mental functions, was very fundamental in maintaining the integrity and pre-eminence of psychoanalysis over many attempts to over-shine it or replace it. The most characteristic about the subject is the centrality, supremacy, and the special place the unconscious has in any theoretical configuration of his nature.

Yet, there is no conception of psychoanalytic nature that has been subjected to more modification, reformulation, and was almost rediscovered anew several times, but still remains a puzzle, like the concept of the unconscious. The puzzle is that in spite of no denying of its existence, there is no definite and defined meaning to what the term denotes, even within the psychoanalytic community. It is understandable now that the whole Western culture was waiting for someone to discover that missing part in the veritable theories of the subject. Even after Freud discovered it and opened the impasse that the philosophers reached, the problem is not fully resolved. Freud started with the simple notion of repression of objectionable conscious ideas or desires. After that early and modest beginning, he realized that there is more to 'forgetting' something than making a conscious element *unconscioused.*

Hence, he proceeded and differentiated between three possible meanings to the term unconscious: a descriptive meaning (an objective), a dynamic meaning (a subject), and a systemic meaning (a condition and a process). The interesting point in that third vein is that psychoanalysts – in particular – are still puzzling about while non-analysts (artist in particular) got its core connotation easily and just after Freud's first three works on the normal subject.

The first two types of unconsciousness are creations of a process of making something recede from consciousness. The conscious material that is pushed out of consciousness becomes descriptively unconscious. If recalling it faces memory resistance it could be called dynamically unconscious, because of its interaction with opposing forces of recall. However, the existence of a third systemic *Ucs.* was uncontestable. The most intra-psychical phenomena like psychoneuroses and dreams were not explainable by the two simplistic mechanisms of repression and difficulties of recall. Interpreting a dream proves that it is not about something that deserved to be repressed or that it is about an objectionable disturbing content. Dream work, which creates the format of wishing in a dream, happens without the dreamer's intent, expectation, or ability to disguise his wishes. Interpretation shows that dream work is a process that disguises a wish or an intention in a way that makes it consciously unrecognizable; *the unconscious that is not a result of repression is a result of the working of the primary process in disguising it.* In the *Irma* dream, the construction of the scene of the great physicians making fools of themselves happened unconsciously and merely *disguised* Freud's wish to prevail over them. There was no consciousness turned into unconsciousness in that part of the dream, but there was a system that worked during sleep to create a representation of a wish, i.e., any wish. Freud (1912g) explained this third meaning as follows: "The system [unconscious] revealed by the sign that the single acts forming parts of it are unconscious. We designate by the name 'the unconscious,' for want of a better and less ambiguous term. In German, I proposed to denote this system by the letters *Ubw*, an abbreviation of the German word 'unbewusst.' *And this is the third and most significant sense which the term unconscious has acquired in psychoanalysis* (emphasis added)" (266).

The systemic unconscious is the real and most important of all the Freudian discoveries. Up to the moment he came to that concept there was no hint in his work to suggest that he thought of the unconscious outside the framework of repression or a cognitive meaning. Thus, it is puzzling not to have any point of reference to go back to, to understand where the *systemic unconscious* came from or related to. This puzzle had to wait for eleven more years to be put in context. When he was putting together, presumably his last theory of the psyche (the structural point of view) he made a major fiasco. He tried to assign psychical functions to psychical agencies, like assigning to the *Id* containing of the instincts and the repressible conscious material, and to consider the ego the seat of consciousness. Unexpectedly he had a sudden significant new insight; realizing that a part of the ego was unconscious too. He said (1923 b): "A part of the ego too – and heaven knows how important a part – may be *Ucs.*, undoubtedly is *Ucs.,* and this *Ucs.* belonging to the ego is not latent like the *Pcs.*; if it were it could not be activated without becoming *Cs.*, and the process of making it conscious would not encounter such great difficulty. When we find ourselves thus confronted by the necessity of postulating a third *Ucs.*, which is not repressed, we must admit that *the characteristic of being unconscious begins to lose significance (*my emphasis*)*. It becomes a quality which can have many meanings, a quality which we are unable to make, which we have hoped to do, the basis of far-reaching and inevitable conclusions" (18).

To make the reification of the structural point of view work, Freud had to implant a segment of the topographic model in its agencies. He realized that it is not possible to assign *functions* to agencies (structures) that are not initially related or had something in common. Hence, he attached to each of the agencies a mini topographic tripartite system. This gesture was obviously a temporary band-aid, because the systemic unconscious was to become the real and the permanent solution. The real unconscious is the non-repressed unconscious because it is not conditional on the theory adopted or the school followed.

The idea of unconsciousness within the sphere of consciousness sounds at a first glance paradoxical. How could unconscious thoughts be present in consciousness without being noted and recognized? Yet, the non-repressed unconscious is a common feature in our daily life, and we seldom pay attention to. Sophocles' *Oedipus Rex* was enjoyed by audiences all over the world and in different times in history. No one (till Freud) became conscious of its unconscious meaning and its individual psychical importance and appeal. The Oedipus complex is unconscious within humanity's consciousness, since Abraham's attempt to kill his son to please God. We find another example of non-repressed unconscious in our ordinary daily speech. We speak our native languages with just adequate syntax and bare knowledge of its correct grammar. Yet, even an uneducated person would still notice a grammatical mistake made by a non-native speaker. The grammar of our spoken language is unconscious though it dictates most of our conscious speech and acts. The most puzzling about the non-repressed unconscious is the extent of its presence in our collective conscious life, without giving a hint to its existence. Wars, in particular religious wars, have conscious justifications that are offered to distract from the unconscious falsies offered to instigate them. More examples could be given regarding the ego's unconscious and conscious deceptions that are created to distract from the truth, because many of their manifestations have only unconscious functions. Point in fact, the role of repression in forming the preconscious is clear and understandable, but if we tried to define a function for repression or its place in the system *Ucs.* we will be lost in finding even something tangible to suggest its workings.

It took Freud three more years to explain the absent role of repression in the formation of the systemic *Ucs.*, In 1915 Freud offered a totally new statement about repression, which – in hindsight – was the explanation of the non-repressed unconscious. In that year Freud published his 'metapsychological papers' of which one was dedicated to repression. In it he differentiated between two types of repressions: *primal* repression and repression *proper*. 'Primal repression' dealt with early material that pertains to the preverbal and early stages of undefined experiences of the infant goes through as a subject. The material of primal repression is fundamentally the affective aspects of those experiences. They have no verbal concomitants or are associated with cognitive memories. Those experiences get formed early and remain psychically contentless. In this meaning those are the material that belongs to the systemic unconscious. Clinical work has shown that those early experiences could latch on to some of the more recent conceptions, affective reactions, and vague experiences, and usurp their significance and manage to enter consciousness. When they do that, they confuse consciousness. Most the hazy and isolated affective states are material from the primarily repressed process. They are *aconscious*. For reasons that he left for us to entertain Freud called that type of repression primal and not primary (Fayek, 2014). The second repression or the familiar repression that Freud called 'repression proper' deals with material that has been conscious for a while but without any representation that could be managed by the secondary processes, thus had to be repressed later as a 'defensive' measure.

Clinically, the most difficult to interpret is the material of primal repression, because even if the analyst forms ideas about it, it still remains a problem to find the proper meaning that could respond to interpreting it. For example, castration phantasies express primal narcissistic injuries that get linked to them later in development, almost like an after-effect case. The manifestation of castration fears is not possible to trace back to when they were assimilated in infancy. The fears of being abandoned, neglected, and humiliated would get attached to the notion of castration a little later (the Oedipus position). What we get of that early primal repression is the social and conventional representations of humiliation that are associated with castration.

Another example comes from a lady who complained of being compulsively argumentative (others also complained of that characteristic in her). She mentioned in a casual way (sort of a screen memory) watching her father being chastised by his older sister for something she did not know. She wanted – very much – to defend her (remembers the affective pain and frustration) at that time but couldn't. Bringing this memory in context of her argumentative nature recalled several infantile feelings and sensations of restriction in church, gatherings of adults at home, and other situation that required of her to be proper. Primal repression forced the repressed to link with life events and situations that gave it a chance to be re-expressed. Argumentativeness was a wish in the past and became a mode of relating in adulthood.

The maturation of the theory of psychoanalysis allowed Freud to bypass the difficulties he encountered with the concept of the unconscious. Instead of dealing with the rich concept of the unconscious, he made changes to the concept of repression which revealed some major attributes of the systemic unconscious. Matte-Blanco (1988) believed that most psychoanalysts did not understand properly the systemic unconscious, and the result was confusing it with the descriptive and the dynamic meanings. It could be added that even Freud did not adhere to its different meanings all the time. He sometimes leaned toward the two other functional meanings of the unconscious. He assigned to both some contents, such as sexuality and instinctual impulses, and used them mostly to interpret psychosocial phenomena. Thereby, every time he did that, he revoked the significance of the structural qualifications of the unconscious. He overlooked what he had previously stipulated regarding the wish's links with the *Cs-Pcs.* systems, which allows it to lose its quality as a systemic unconscious. Minimizing the importance of all those elements that were central to his intuition about unconsciousness made him sometimes retreat to the unconscious as a product of defense mechanisms, which works essentially in the service of the ego.

The Solution of the Puzzle

The difficulties Freud encountered with 'unconsciousness' were due to the link that he previously established between repression and the unconscious, and kept its shadow on his mind (and most analysts) for a long time. Everything that was later discovered about the unconscious was practically correcting the flawed theory of repression. The cathartic theory imposed a shadow on most of the new psychoanalytic discoveries (Fayek, 2013). The existence of psychical material in a state of unconsciousness regardless of going through the process of repression or not forced Freud to revisit and revise the concept of repression itself so he would not do away with it completely. In other words, Freud seems to have assumed that the problem of settling the concept of the unconscious could happen within the concept of repression. He had the intuition, though, that there could be two types of repression: repression proper which is the same old concept that turns something conscious to unconsciousness, and a process of repression that deals with material from very early phases in life, or material that is un-transformable to mental representations that could be submitted to repression proper. I believe that Freud realized – after recognizing the extent of the workings of the primary process and its role in the formation of psychical life in general – that the unconscious is an essential and built-in process in every psychological aspect of the subject's life, and it is not just an incidental event in odd psychoneurosis. In other word, the unconscious is not a casual state that could happen or not happen in psychical events. The unconscious is the antithesis of consciousness, therefor, there must be something similar to 'repression proper' that allowed consciousness to start forming from the moment consciousness was initiated. Thus, primal repression has to be active from the beginning of the birth of the function of consciousness.

Consciousness relies on reaching a sense of meaning to keep functioning consistently and in coordination with memory. Primal repression, an active primitive process in the pre-meaning stage, facilitates letting the psychological external reality to initiate consciousness. A hungry enfant needs to repress his anger at the delay in feeding him in order to become conscious of the breast – when it is offered – and to start feeding. Anger could be primly repressed, but is likely to emerge at any future delay in satisfying the needs of that enfant in his adulthood. Freud gave that process the name *primal* repression, which answers to the contradictions of a non-repressed unconscious (1923 b). In other terms, Freud needed to find a mechanism that explains psychical material that becomes active without entering the system *Psc-Cs*.

Something has to be underlined in regards to primal repression. Consciousness has no reference to reality, and as a process that is without an identified reference would always give the impression of a personal and subjective matter, i.e., the specifics of that particular person. Primal repression, deals with the preverbal experiences of that particular individual and maintains them as background of many psychical events that will happen later to that person. They become the source and point of reference of consciousness in that person. In that manner, the primarily repressed constitutes several aspects of the psychical life of the subject. Phantasies are one of those aspects. For instance, preverbal experiences like breastfeeding are primarily repressed and preserved as a 'modality' for certain new aspects of the intrapsychic life. Those preverbal experiences are assigned to memory but remained as pre-memory structures. They are kept as the background for the ensuing experiences of any lack and fulfillment, which are intrinsic experiences of the oral phase. The primarily repressed lurks in the background as a past experience that awaits a present event (like un-fulfillment) to get some access to consciousness. In a way, *primal repression is not the opposite of repression proper: it facilitates the past to get access to consciousness, while the other prevents the present from having access to consciousness.* They complement each other.

The revision of the concept of repression and discovering what could create the non-repressed unconscious was supposed to be a major shift in the direction of psychoanalysis. The three papers of 1914 (c, d, e) reveal Freud's wish to give his theory a firm basis in psychology (those three papers are psychological points of view and not metapsychological, as Strachey claimed in the editor's note in Standard Edition). It was possible, with the new concepts of the non-repressed unconscious and primal repression to talk about the psychodynamics of the subject's intrapsychic instead of talking about the psychodynamic of the conscious psychical events, processes, issue, etc. Unfortunately, Freud's background as a physician and his reluctance to consider psychoanalysis an extension of the intellectual movement of the nineteen and twentieth century, or as a human science, made him miss that chance to position psychoanalysis properly within the general wave of discoveries in the humanities.

Chapter Nine

Reconstituting the Subject

The Subject Matter of Psychoanalysis

The thinkers of the age of philosophy (see chapter three) discovered substantial and essential attributes of the human subject[1]. However, they could not put their discoveries together to come up with a theory of the subject. They knew that 'something' in the cognitive manifestations of the subject is missing but could not specify what it could be. Freud on the other hand discovered the unconscious, and in its most basic nature, but did not establish the link between his findings and the findings of the philosophers. The reason as was suggested in chapter one is the nature of functional theories that have no conception of the structural theories. The findings of philosophy are structural in essence, while Freud's efforts were mainly functional explanations for his finds. What we have now is two great masses of knowledge about the subject, with some operational ideas of the link and the absence of the link that manifests in psychopathological symptoms. Actually, the link is between the subject as

---

[1] Before giving serious attention to the clinical aspect of psychoanalysis and deciding on getting the training and the qualification of practicing, I studied the available psychoanalytic literature with great interest and concentration, because I found the theory to be very vital for clinical psychologists and the academic teaching of general psychology. When I got the chance to get training in a recognized institute, I had some reservations about limiting the theoretical training to the technicalities of psychoanalyzing. When I felt more confident in what I learned of psychoanalysis I gradually realized that knowing the theory well is not just essential for practice; it differentiate between two types of psychoanalysts. There is practice of psychoanalysis as a profession, and psychoanalyzing as an act of rearranging the psychical structure of a subject. It took some more time to realize that not knowing the theory well is what makes the difference, but learning about the subject that psychoanalyzing reveals to us is what improves practice. It is undeniable that psychoanalytic training now is not giving this difference much consideration.

partially known (philosophy) and partially explained (psychoanalysis). We need to reconstitute our findings in a way that would allow explaining the findings. Doing that, at this stage of discovering and interpreting the dual nature of the subject requires the group efforts of serious analysts like Bion, Laplanche, Green, Matte-Blanco, Lacan, Kohut, and few more who dug out of psychopathology the normal attributes of the subject's psyche.

The Subject in a Structural Theory

I tried till now to show that the 'subject' has been the subject matter of Western philosophy since Descartes imparted his Cogito. The basic issue in both the philosophers' endeavors and Freud's are how the concept of the unconscious could help reveal the nature of the subject; Intrapsychic. A structural approach to the subject was born out of realizing that there is no conscious attribute that could be understood without finding an obviously missing component in it. The more Freud exposed the unconscious features the more it became clear that there is difference between two psychoanalyses: functional and structural psychoanalyses. Functional psychoanalyzing is a psychology of explanation, while, structural psychoanalysis is based on interpreting psychical phenomena as constructs of *Cs.* and *Ucs.* The distinction between the two psychoanalyses is our guiding rule in identifying psychoanalysis as a theory of the subject, because the structural model of theoretical thinking has become – generally speaking – the exclusive way of approaching the phenomena of the subject in the humanities in general. No sociologist, anthropologist, psychologist, moralist, etc., would concentrate on subjects of the issue he is researching; they all look for the phenomena and study it to interpret its individual states. Freud did not study the dreamers but interpreted the phenomena of dreaming.

In chapter one I made a distinction between a psychoanalytic theory of the subject and psychoanalysis as *a* theory of the subject. I repeat this point here because after reviewing the psychoanalytic findings about the subject, such as duality, wishing, sexuality, narcissism, the unconsciousness, etc., we come to ask: were those attributes unknown before psychoanalysis and could psychoanalysis be the only discipline that discovered them? Those attributes were known before but out of context, and psychoanalysis succeeded in giving them that missing context. The subject's attributes are *denotations* of some specific features in the subject; therefore, *psychoanalysis is a theory of the subject not a psychoanalytic theory of the subject.* In other terms, *psychoanalysis is not the discovery of the attributes of the subject; it is discovering what the attributes of the subject reveal of his nature.*

Psychoanalysis was a novelty and quite an intuitive way of understanding dreams, wits, phobias, etc., and to read in those attributes unnoticeable and confusing matters about the psychical life of the subject. Missing or forgetting this distinction is responsible for the deterioration of psychoanalysis and limiting it to a technique (s) of psychotherapy. A theory of the subject places psychoanalysis in the context of the general theory of the humanities. It will also answer to another implicit issue that is usually raised by the clinical psychoanalysis: is psychoanalysis an application of dealing with the subject, or does the subject demand a psychoanalytic way of thinking to deal with him properly[2]? In a more direct way: is Freud's so-called classical psychoanalysis dead or is it still alive?

The 'subject' as concept is not a psychoanalytic discovery; it is a philosophical one. Freud's fifty years of work on the subject was a project in progress and the discovery of the subject was in the making all that time in psychoanalysis and the humanities. In this chapter I chose three attributes of the subject and their specific interconnections to show that psychoanalysis as a theory of the subject deals with 'his' nature, not some of his attributes. I will try to show that the attributes of the subject complements each other in a consistent way, but when they do not, they create the psychoneurotic conditions clinical analysts name a psychoanalysis. The three attributes I chose are linked in a clear structural way, which makes it possible, easy, and proper to consider them the core of a right theory of the subject. A theory of the subject is to be of *what* is he, not *how and why* he is what he is. The subject as the duo of thinking and being cannot be considered anymore an entity, but a psychical event that is to be considered as of a dual nature. The continuous interaction between the duo of the subject keeps the splitting of consciousness rejuvenating itself, accept the coexistence of consciousness and unconsciousness, and many more divisions that are assumed till now as epistemological entities.

The separation the Cogito envisaged allows putting the findings of psychoanalysis in a more identifiable way. The subject as a creature of dualities is now more understandable than before when he was seen as a unity or an entity. Psychoanalysis, in that sense, is a theory of the ongoing interaction between its component and the processes that give the subject the distinction of being the primate who is not ruled by instinct, but the one that generate

---

[2] It is important in emphasizing that psychoanalysis is not a clinical discipline but a theory of everything that pertains to the subject. Psychoanalysis is capable of providing substantial input in understanding social, political, historical and most of the other human phenomena.

mental representations of his instinctual base and responds to what he created out of his needs. The simple fact that the subject is dualities makes us look for the most central, basic, and encompassing dualities that could explain the existence of the rest of the dualities.

What could distinguish a duality to supersede another is its links with the other dualities. A duality that is essential for other dualities to exist should be considered more basic and encompassing. For instance, the duality *I-me* is more encompassing than the one of conscious\unconscious, because the former causes the latter and not the other way around. For that reason, I started with the basic split underlined in the Cogito of *I* think that links with *me* which the *I* brings to being. This duality leads to the duality of the manifest-latent because *me* is unconsciously the content of *I*. This functional link leads to the next sensible duality of the conscious-unconscious.

Three Basic Dualities

1. I and Me Duality

The duality of the body and the mind was the most basic and the earliest in the history of the subject's notion of his-self. However, after the subject invented language to first express himself, and secondly to know what the other is about, and thirdly to turn a need into a wish, the body/mind duality gave most of its significance to the duality of *I/me*. As the duality of body-mind is neither unconscious nor preconscious but infuses the subject's sense of being, the duality of *I-me* created unconscious representations of the subject, the other, and the objects. It did that in the form of pronouns (Fayek, 2002). This is maybe the greatest invention that allowed speech to quickly develop into languages. On a smaller scale we see similar developmental steps guiding the child's acquisition of language. Moreover, with some attention to the evolution of a process of psychoanalyzing we could also notice changes in the patient's associations (language of the unconscious) suggesting mastering self-expression better.

The duality of *I-me* is more complicated than the simple duality of body/mind because it deals with the subject's speech, not just his sense of being. The subject's speech is a complex act that expresses him in both his capacities as a subject to the self and an object to the other, revealing thus another unique human feature: *the subject could speak to the other as an I, and about himself to the same other but as a me.* This duality created a problem for Freud, and to other analyst, because they had to make a distinction between the subject of the act of analysis and the subject of the theory of analysis. Freud chose the term *Ego* to denote the speaking subject and the spoken-about object.

So, it was common to find confusing statements about the speaking ego and the spoken about ego. Both egos replaced the subject and *him* as an object. Using the term ego did not solve any problems; it created a confusion because it implicitly denoted the person as a whole (self and body), and explicitly as a particular part of the mind that has certain functions and characteristics (Strachey's editor's introduction to *The Ego and the Id* (1923, b).

Precluding the distinction between the subject and the object looked in the literature as a good solution to the problem of talking clinically about the patient. Analysts took the liberty to refer to the patient as an ego, thus can report on the changes and the doings of the ego without clear distinction between what they observed clinically and what they thought theoretically. Ego psychology was a retreat to the *pre-psychoanalysis psychoanalysis* when the subject was an epistemological entity. Psychologically speaking we could use ego to mean the person as an object and functions. However, psychoanalytically, we are not supposed to ignore the difference because we are always referring to the patient in the context of his definition of himself. A third problem with ego-psychology was not offering a suggestion to a solution. The Ego was used in the third unrelated context of *narcissism* to mean the self (neither *I* nor *me)*. Laplanche and Pontalis (1973) were against using terms – like ego – that could have more than one meaning, depending on the context it is used in, like objectifying libidinal investment. The idea is that ego should have one definite connotation if we decided to give it a 'theoretical value.' I would also add now that after several decades of Ego-psychology the the term *ego* was eventually severed from every other qualification it had, and was reified and rendered a meaningless term that annulled the duality of the *I* and *me*. Ego became a psychoanalytic entity in its own right. To reposition the duality of *I-me,* in a theory of the subject I would say that Descartes' cogito puts the subject within this duality without specifying a causal link between *I* think and I *am* 'me' who does the thinking.

Psychoanalysis seized to be a theory of the subject when analysts were tempted to think of psychoanalyzing as a 'procedure' like medical procedures. It was natural, therefore, to change psychoanalysis into a theory of an entity called the Ego. Strachey's translation turned the subject into an object of a vague meaning and eliminated the subjectivity that is latent in the *I*. Analysts stopped thinking and talked about the subject as a living entity and thought and talked of him as an object, where 'certain' psychical events take place and happen. An example taken from a well-known paper on the process of analysis the author saying: "…once the patients grasp the analytic task of attempting to verbalize to the analyst whatever appears on the stage of consciousness, their egos become *continuously* alert to the danger of 'too much' exposure." This sentence expresses fittingly something that was regularly envisaged as real clinical experience when it was merely verbalization of an imaginary process in practicing. It is not the patient's ego that reacts to the gradual change in awareness; it is *he* who reacted to changes in his awareness. Is there a difference! Yes, the mere replacement of the patient with 'ego' changes the essence and substance of the psychoanalytic act; analysis becomes an act of analyzing *an object* or something in the subject or what happens to the subject as a function of him as an object. Even if we manage to effect some change in that thing (aggression!) in isolation of the rest of the subject we cannot claim we did psychoanalytic work, because we do not do changes in aggression, we change the aggressive subject.

The change in the attitude toward psychoanalysis as a procedure was lauded by psychoanalysts in the school of ego-psychology, and infiltrated to the other schools that leaned toward having something to identify them. They preferred analyzing an object like the ego, the super ego, inter-subjectivity, rather than analyzing the patient. This could be put in a different way: analyst seem to have preferred discovering the *unconscious* in a manifestation of the subject (interrelationships, intersubjective interaction, demands for the affection, regrets and sadness, etc.) than deducing it directly from the patients' speech. This distinction makes the duality of the *I-me* of a particular psychoanalytic significance: establishing that *Ego* is the translation of the subjective pronoun *I* and regarding the *'me'* the objective pronoun of the subject we can identify who is talking to us in the session: the patient or what he thinks of himself.

The duality of the *I-me* is the main structuring base in human communication; it is the fabric of language. Without it verbal and non-verbal exchanges would be unintelligible because speaking would not reveal the natural and expected intentionality of the speaker: *who is talking to whom about what*. Better, without the means of differentiating between the speaker and the intended listener to the spoken message, speech loses the purpose of talking. The situation gets more complex when the message is about a third subject. Although the pronouns are the effective tool in making the third subject distinct from the two speakers (*I* and *me*), this distinction is not always easy especially if the third party who is spoken about is one of the two speakers. This situation is of marked importance in a psychoanalytic session: is the subject talking about a present object or a transference object!

Clinically speaking, the distinction between the subject and the object in the patient's speech is important enough that it could be part of assessing the degree of improvement achieved in analysis. The importance of that distinction and underlining it is related to what I think happened to psychoanalysis after the ego lost its usefulness in revealing the unconscious, and after the deterioration of ego psychology. This distinction allows differentiating between a relation with the analyst and the transference relation. Because the *me* is the patient talking, it is in a transferential relationship with the analysts, while the *I* is able only of relating to the actualities of the relationship with the analyst.

The emergence of the relational schools as replacement for ego psychology caused another change in the technique and the practice of analytic therapy. Analysts abandoned the Freudian tripartite protocol of practice and replaced it with 'real' relations to the patients. Consequently, it became less important to consider transference a valid way to recover unconscious material and childhood memories. The three elements of the Freudian protocol of anonymity, neutrality, and abstinence (see chapter eleven) are means to an end and not simply just recommendations that we are free to ignore.

In relational psychoanalysis the difference between interpretation and explanation was ignored because the unconscious was no longer *deduced* from the patient's transference association, but presumably was embedded in relationships. This change caused analysts to miss an evident fact: a relationship employs both the *I* and the *me,* in a mixture of primary and secondary processes Therefore, the act of psychoanalyzing which is supposed to translate one language to another would not have the distinction needed in the patient's rhetoric. (see Freud, 1910k).

Translation could simple be by replacing the vocabulary of a text with the vocabulary of another language. This kind of translation uses a simple process of making the new vocabulary *explain* the original vocabulary. Analysts and sometimes some patients translate manifest material by another manifest material (preconscious material to conscious material). Explaining a patient's anger at his wife as combining and expressing his previously frustrated anger at his mother exemplify this kind of psychoanalytic translation. Another kind of translation is finding the subtle and disguised meaning in the terminology used in the original text and revealing it – in not an exact equivalent vocabulary in the other language – but find the appropriate vocabulary in the new language that reveals the disguised meaning. This kind of translation *interprets* the text in the new language. Interpretation turns the analyst's work into a process of making the patient's text a meaningful issue. A clinical vignette could show that distinction better:

A patient was quite sure of understanding one of his characteristics: a compulsive trend to take the opposite position in any discussion. He stated that he cannot stop himself arguing anything and everything that is brought to his attention. He *explained* his compulsion to argue as expressing his deep believes that nothing is absolute and there is relativity in everything. I pointed out that arguing compulsively will sometimes make him take the wrong position without intending to do that. He argued with me saying that he only argues to show that there could be other points of view not necessarily to convince the adversary. Noticing that he was arguing with me, he realized that he *precociously* took a personal rigid attitude of being an advocate of causes. This line of associations led to a preconscious construct relating to his parents' who constantly bickered. This new twist revealed that arguing was not purely an intellectual position or a moral or ethical act, but a personal attribute. The analyst said something to the effect that the explanation he gave shows that he had an attitude that formed as a reaction to personal experiences. He was faced with the fallacy that he was compulsive in arguing, and realized that he does that for a particular childhood formation. The patient was surprised that he did not notice the contradiction in his explanations (the emergence of something unconscious in his conscious logic!) What his *I* was saying consciously about his intentions was not truly him (*me*). He was unconsciously dealing with issues that pertain to his particular history. What he seemed to complain of was translating something else that deserved translating.

Patients' explanations are different from the ones the analyst sometimes uses; they are more rationalizations than explanations, they could be repetitions of meanings given to their behavior by others. The explanations given by the analyst are reformulations of what the patient has already said, given back to the patient to highlight some preconscious content in his statement. The analyst could use reformulating the patient's explanations to establish – in the patient – a sense that his explanations carry more meaning than what appears, thus pave the way to the process of interpretation. Those reformulations still address the causes given by the patient but they highlight the possibility of the existence of a meaning or intent behind the explanation or the rationalizations. Explanations, when done properly and timely free the *I* from its adhesion to the *Cs./Pcs.* system. Listening carefully to the patient's explanations, with *attention to the words* he uses would reveal that the patient is unconsciously elucidating a dormant infantile *me*. The duality of *I-me* makes the patient 'say' things that serve other meanings. The patient's explanations are the manifest of something latent.

2. The Manifest and the Latent Duality

Even if there is no agreement on one explanation of homosapien invention of language we should not ignore the idea itself. The lack of exact correspondence between *I* and *me* was a major factor in the creation of speech as a constituent of language. It explains – in any way it is taken – a very central aspect of psychological life. Every indication of psychological life is comprised of its manifest presence and a latent meaning within it. The *I* expresses the subject's presence or existence but it does not mean anything if it; it does not reveal its latent content. The latent of the *I* is the first duality of the subject of psychoanalysis.

The duality of the manifest and the latent is seldom noticed in human behavior or even recognized as a duality because of its implicit existence in the very act of talking. *The Interpretation of Dreams* (Freud,1900a) – the first legitimate psychoanalytic work – introduced the notion of the manifest dream and the latent content of the manifest. It was, by all measures, the most accepted duality in everything related to our discipline. The proof to that duality did not raise any reservations from analysts and non-analysts. In the *Irma* dream, Freud's wish to exonerate himself of making a mistake in the diagnosis is a legitimate wish of all physicians, not only Freud. The anger at the medical profession that was belittling his endeavors was also 'not a crime to hide.' Even the megalomaniac extent of the two latent ideas that created the dream was not enough to create such an elaborate disguise of the two latent contents.

Freud started psychoanalysis from the notion of a conflict between two wishes: one acceptable and one unacceptable. We should keep our attention focused on the way opposing wishes fit within the duality of the manifest\latent. Do conflicting wishes conflict in their manifest expression or latent content? The reason we should pay attention to this point is that we, psychoanalysts, are not supposed to with conflict between wishes but conflict between the manifest and the latent of the wishes.

A wish, or better the state of wishing, tells of a gap between a manifest, which the subject could easily identify, but is not as easy to define its content. In the *Irma* dream, Freud was quick and not hesitant in identifying his anxiety and resentment to Otto's implicit criticism of his treatment of *Irma*. The manifest and the latent were clearly connected. Nevertheless, Freud as a mature responsible physician should not have blamed those physicians for their bias to the degree expressed in the dream. The latent content of the wish of the night before the dream linked with the latent content of the childhood wish to produce that elaborate gathering of silly physicians. *The duality of the manifest and the latent is a duality that permits, if not encourage, arbitrary fusions between contents of different manifest phenomena, even from different times.* In the *Irma* dream Freud had no control over the process of creating the manifest of his wish but he chose its latent content and found for it in a previous event. The separation of the manifest and the latent in a psychical phenomenon is usually – if not always – the event that encourages arbitrary combinations of wishes and styles of fulfilling them. This is the basis of the psychoneuroses.

Psychoanalysts got distracted by the existence of the gap between the manifest and the latent because the Freudian work on dreams and parapraxes became the model to use in discovering the unconscious. However, such gap happens in normal and abnormal conditions in the same way. The difference is in the subject's own specific way of dealing with that gap. It is a gap that could be the scene of creative outcomes as well as unfortunate failures. Because this gap is a structural element in the subject's dealing with 'his' self it should be looked at as the state of affairs in any psychological phenomena. The simplest way to formulate a theory of the subject is to say that *the subject is whoever lay between his manifest givens and their latent contents*. The subject's health and sickness, his character formation and deformation, his potentials and lack of it, all are constructs of the way the *he* is filling that gap by his own views about them and through the workings of the primary process that forces itself on the process.

Analysts who apply theoretical frameworks that seem to fit the material miss the point, even if they are right in their choice. Psychoanalyzing is working with the patient on the gap between the manifest and the latent – as his subjective gap – and not a given we could provide. We should keep in mind Freud's thesis (1916–17 a) that the first reaction the subject takes in responding to an endosomatic stimulus is to *represent* the stimulus in mind because the response is going first to the psychical representation and not to the stimulus. A sense of deprivation and lack of fulfilment could be represented in the mind by a craving for something edible, followed by acting upon hunger or thirst.

Freud's insight of the reciprocity between mind and body in humans was the basis of the concept of *Trieb*. He said (1915c): "I am in fact of the opinion that the antithesis of conscious and unconscious is not applicable to instinct [*Trieb*]. An instinct can never become an object of consciousness only an idea that represents the instinct can... If the instinct did not attach itself to an idea [in the *Pcs.*] or manifest itself as an affective state, we could not know anything about it (p. 177) [it would remain *Ucs.*]." Therefore, doing analysis should always maintain that the link between the manifest and the latent is not fixed, is not the same all the time, and is arbitrary, depending on the events of the that part of this particular session.

Usually analysts consider the manifest the equivalent of the conscious and the latent is unconscious. This understanding has a serious flaw because the latent always exists in consciousness and has no other place to be. The issue is it exists in a disguised way that makes its consciousness misleading. If the latent has no presence in consciousness, it would be impossible to reach it and relate the manifest to it. Moreover, if the latent is unconscious we would not be able to find in consciousness its manifest. Therefore, a blind belief in the correspondence of the manifest to consciousness and the latent to unconsciousness depicts two flawed dualities.

3. The Conscious-Unconscious Duality

In chapter seven, the duality of the conscious and the unconscious was discussed from the point of view of clarifying the concept of the unconscious. The emphasis was put on the unconscious as a systemic construct of the intrapsychic and the foundation of the psychical life of the subject. This viewpoint would conflict with the still prevailing idea in contemporary psychoanalysis that the unconscious has to be forced out of consciousness, or at best is not the main issue in psychoanalysis, unless it interferes with what is considered more relevant to what the works on the unconscious as 'the condition' which describes the state of affairs in the intrapsychic life of the subject conflicts strongly with the prevailing attitude that it is some psychical material that psychoanalyzing will ultimately take care of, whether it is part of relational matters or an element of the intersubjective relationship with others. This is the attitude of most clinical psychoanalysts of the day. They pursue the work of analysis with a vision of the unconscious as psychical interference in the natural psychological phenomena. More striking is the absence in those theoretical stances of any clear understanding of the two issues of reconstruction and termination. What could lead to and decide if the analysis has come to its end?

Revealing infantile sexuality and amnesia clarifies symptom formation and changes the unconscious from 'some repressed morally debatable urges' to a presence of aspects of sexuality in adult life that never entered consciousness to be targeted by repression. They remained target for the processes that would disguises them and render them unconscious. The unconscious in this case is the process that disguises the latent and sets up misleading manifestations that make the latent content systemically unconscious. A vignette could explain this point. A patient reveals in her analysis a preoccupation with what her lover thinks of her frigidity. She was frigid in her sexual relations with men, though she did not feel that way when masturbating. The relation between sexual manifestation and their latent content were determined by childhood sexual events that she recalls. The relation between the *I* am a woman and the *me* is a child was the crux of the conflict. The gradual and persistent work through recovered memories and revealing their childhood meanings led to a termination of the continuous referring the present sexuality to infantile sexuality. Analysis would not have terminated successfully if the guilt and shame of infantile sexuality was not interpreted in order to undergo change.

The evolution of the concept 'unconscious' and the insights regarding its nature matched the increasing knowledge of the intrapsychic. This point raises a subtle question: does 'unconsciousing' psychical things create intrapsychic life, or is the intrapsychic life unconscious by its nature?

In chapter three, the duality of the *I-me* was considered the basic unavoidable narcissistic structure of the subject. Psychoanalysts expect of the patient to 'free associate' in order for the freely speaking *I-me* duality reveals the unconscious that is implicit in the subject's speech. For the subject to free associate he is supposed to suppress the *I* to let the *me* do the talking. So, asking the subject to free associate is asking him to do something primarily impossible (not to be his narcissistic self, or suppress the observing *I*). The transcendence of consciousness would – in a natural way – interrupt associating freely because the *I* is incapable of objectifying itself fully without omitting, falsifying, and misrepresenting the self. However, the speech of the patient – as a patient – exposes the duality of the *I-me*, yet in a different way. Free association happens when the subject manages to do what the analyst asked him to do: *not* to talk about what he knows but to talk *in order* to know the *me* that will reveal itself. Interpretations, on the other hand, deal with the *intention* (meaning) of the psychical event, not the cause or the content of what is said. The intention of the psychic event is what the mature *I-me* duality should say or do if it were not obstructed by the infantile *me*, or a neurotic structure. The intention of the psychical event is entwined with the event itself (the manifest), and the patient does not notice that it is the latent of the event he is talking about. In other words, an interpretation shows what should have been said (revealed) if the dormant *I* did not have the power to impose its will on the situation. For that reason, it could be said that *interpretations do not follow (should not follow) any theoretical lines or lead to any theoretical verifications, because they are merely deduced from what is expressed, even from what was not said by the patient, and was just insinuated.* The best material that carries the unconscious openly and quite convincingly is transference material (Fayek, 2017). In transference, the gap between the *me* and the *I* gets reoriented toward the present, i.e. the analytic situation.

It is important that the analyst preserves more than a modicum of the Freudian protocol to give transference the needed space to emerge and develop into a one-sided relationship with the analyst, instead of an interaction. It is well agreed that the psychoanalytical situation engenders the phenomenon of transference. Transference is unconsciously activated by the analyst's neutrality and abstinence, therefore the return of the past to be relived in the present entails some changes in the duality of the *I-me*, and a great deal of changes in the duality of *I-he*. The confusion of identities in the transference situation, particularly because the subject's continuous changing – as a response to the analyst's work of interpretation – reveals a characteristic of the subject that deserves more attention than it usually gets. *Transference is not a psychoanalytic phenomenon or a phenomenon of psychoanalysis. It is a phenomenon of the subject.* The subject is incapable of having pure new *I-me* duality for new situations of daily events. The subject has a dormant *I-me* duality that is established sometime in his past, in the early years of his formation, and that is what he will face the present with. This formation becomes the prototype of the *I-me* of his new situations, and affects its function accordingly. Depending on the degree of *I-me* definiteness and rigidity, the subject's own free identity and the demands of the present situation, the subject's dormant *I-me* will not activate in all new events. Thus, psychoanalysis as a method of therapy needs to have a way to reveal the patient's *I-me* duality so both analysts and patients could work on the distortions that appear in what the transference reveals.

The subject, who is also an object, and who is epistemologically this duality *in vivo* reveals an underlying quality that is purely psychoanalytic. Although the subject is naturally the same all the time and his *I-me* is supposed to be stable, he is subject to changes according to life situations. However, those changes are always within the range of the duality of the *I-me,* and are rarely serious enough to be considered structural changes. Even if the subject is unstable and shifty, this would be due to an unstable and shifty *I-me* duality.

Chapter Ten
Psychoanalysis: A Science of the Subject

Psychoanalysis has always been in crises since its early beginnings. It started with Alfred Adler and Carl Jung in the first decade of the twentieth century, and there has been no time since without going through a crisis of sorts. This fact takes us to another obvious and related issue. Psychoanalysts seem to have never been alarmed by the crises as long as the crises did not threaten or affect its *international organization*. There was some posturing about psychoanalysis itself at the regional level when the notion of the "schools" emerged. However, when the *IPA* accepted them under its 'big' umbrella the crises seemed to have vanished. For a long period of time, and still, analysts argued and disagreed even split into groups but never came close to genuine intentions to separate from the IPA. Analysts are not eager to articulate their critiques of the other points of view as much as articulating their own points of view. It is obvious that they are not very concerned about psychoanalysis but about its organization.

There are two puzzling issues in such situations which are not easy to note. The disagreements between analysts were about issues of no relevance to psychoanalysis itself. Seldom was there an open argument about the so-called classical theory, even when the argument was clearly about that theory (the British Controversies). Those disagreements were referred to issue about the technicalities of working with transference and interpersonal relations (Kleinian), or ego structure and defenses (Anna Freud). The controversies were very much of a theoretical nature but were downgraded to a difference in technique, and sometimes to personal issues. It could have been looked at as the precursor of the difference between analysis of the intrapsychic and analysis of interpersonal relations, which is problematic till now, but that was not safe then to entertain.

The second feature was leaving the disagreement unresolved, or as Wallerstein (2005) almost recommended silence as an expedient political solution to the crises. It could have been expedient from the political point of view, but not from a practical point of view. A discipline that is developing and evolving needs to firmly define its crises and resolve them. Those crises were about conflicts between old and new points of view, between two conceptions of the classical theory, or replacing the subject matter of the classical theory with a new subject a matter. It was not wise to leave these issues unresolved and contain them within a superficially united institution. The outcome of avoiding confronting the crises was the gradual modifications in the practice of the classical theory that led to the creation of more schools that tempted to replace the defective new schools. Better, theoretical modification of the classical theory was introduced and followed by major changes in the technique of practice (dealing with actual relationships in the analytic scene instead of interpreting transference issues), which led to deceptively calling those changes schools of psychoanalysis.

Freud's attitude and the way he dealt with crises in his time was contributing to their continued existence and proliferation in our time. He was convinced that he is the only one responsible for developing the theory. This attitude was unconsciously assimilated later by all the analyst who assumed leadership positions in the organization of psychoanalysis (Kohut, Lacan etc.). Freud's attitude became the prototype of the disagreements in psychoanalysis, i.e., reluctance to give reasons for disagreeing and improvising new schools. The schools were promoting the new leader's own theory and convictions, and as training analyst he would also guaranty followers. It is expected in every evolving field of knowledge that there will be a line of new leading character, who contributes to that field. The situation in psychoanalysis was different. After Freud's death it took only few years for his prevailing classical theory to fragment into points of view, then into schools. It is easy to explain this change by using a psychoanalytic template that relates the death of the father to n the unity of the family and explain those splits. Yet, what happened is that the newer leaders of psychoanalysis were only eager to usurp the term psycho-analysis for their theoretical views, thus they inherit both the title psychoanalysis and Freud's status of a theoretician together to perpetuate his mistake.

If we ask any professional of what he does he could easily answer depending on what he practices: I am a lawyer, plumber, thinker, or unemployed. The subject matter of the profession defines its title. If a psychoanalyst is asked the same question, he would not find his answer so available. He could reply saying I psychoanalyze patients. But, psychoanalyzing – at the present state of affairs – is not a definite act. Two certified analysts could be doing two quite different things and call them 'psychoanalyzing.' Psychoanalysis, as a profession, has a hypothetical existence or an abstract meaning, but not a concrete subject matter that defines it. The best answer an analyst could come up with at the present time is: *I practice what I was trained to do*. Psychoanalysts are trained in their institutes – in general – to practice clinical work. Freud's theory was the only available 'thing' to define the practice of psychoanalysis for almost half a century. This is no longer the case anymore and there is no single substitute for Freud's theory that could define psychoanalysis. On the contrary, we have almost accepted that there is no longer one psychoanalysis but several psychoanalyses and considered that an improvement. Yet, there is no mention that this is the condition that creates the crises in psychoanalysis in the first place.

Yet, we know now that psychoanalysis is an applicable theory in many areas of human activity. We also know that many human sciences integrated psychoanalysis in their own theoretical body. Analysts are the ones who deny this fact and insist that psychoanalysis is a clinical discipline. The archaic notion that psychoanalysis is the private property of the clinician, and training makes the analysts different and maybe a better person proved to be misleading. Most of what is clinical about psychoanalysis is available and dealt with by the non-clinical professionals, and most of the time in a superior form (see, Foucault 1970, Lacan, Ricoeur, 1971, Straus 1963).

The notion that analysts are the only ones who could understand and practice psychoanalysis because of their training goes back to when personal didactic analysis was the only way to learn analysis. This early and limited view was changed later and after psychoanalysis has permeated our daily life and became a common part of the Western culture. Didactic analysis was changed, even to the clinical psychoanalysts, into therapeutic analysis. This was an attempt to maintain the distinction between psychoanalysts and the non-institute trained people. It is a fact that the crises of psychoanalysis were and are still created by trained and mostly training analysts. The reason is their inability to consider psychoanalysis outside the parochial model of the early times of training. Institute training is presently available only to mental health providers which mean that psychoanalysis is not knowledge to learn, but a skill to acquire to practice a specific profession.

The New Subject of Psychoanalysis

The way clinical psychoanalysis emerged and occupied the whole field of psychoanalysis reflects the basic fault in its evolution. A functional relationship between psychopathology and psychoanalytic findings got established early in the history of psychoanalysis. Freud and Breuer published, maybe, the first work on that subject (1895d). Freud continued to discover few novel things about hysteria, which were also discoveries in the splitting of consciousness. It was established in the late eighteen hundred that psychoanalysis's discoveries are in the field of the psychoneuroses, and its therapy. However, Freud, in a surprising way, published three major works within five years which were not clinical in any way; yet they were the foundation of a psychoanalytic movement. Freud's literature that followed his early functional understanding of psychopathology was non-clinical. Moreover, Freud's clinical work proved to be of poor quality to explain the reputation of psychoanalysis has gained. In the fifty years of his discoveries, insights, and intuitions which changed the field of the humanities beyond any expectations, only one of his clinical works – *The Wolf Man* – has some significance within the psychoanalytic community. On the other hand, most of those intuitions and discoveries had a tremendous effect on the discoveries of the human subject and contributed abundantly to the structural theories of the human subject. The Oedipus complex, narcissism, the workings of the primary process and the *Triebhaft* nature human volition changed the subject from a mere epistemological entity to a dynamic epistemological duality. Freud's psychoanalysis changed the outlook of the subject, society, and most of the ideological believes regarding human nature. It took years – and mostly after Freud's death – for those discoveries to be applied clinically in a proper way, and by fewer numbers that expected.

When the field of psychiatric nosology was expanding – starting from the late forties – there were needs for clarifying and explaining the new and different categories of psychopathology. Differential diagnoses were very central in that process of expansion. Psychoanalysis attempted and successfully made psychopathology a field of discoveries and of giving differential diagnoses new meanings. There was even suggestions and quasi road maps for the psychotherapy of those psychopathologies (Fliess, 1950, 1970). However, the *IPA* kept training as the central issue in the psychoanalytic movement. This stance obstructed shifting the attention from exploring the subject further to restricting psychoanalysis to a practice of psychotherapy. Strangely, limiting psychoanalysis to an act of psychotherapy changed training itself. It went through the natural process, in situations like that, of getting more elaborate, complicated and demanding for no practical reasons, but as the reason for keeping the IPA as the guardian of psychoanalysis.

The notion that training was done in improved institutes that are supervised an accredited by the International Organization turned the whole issue into a licensing process. This change had several serious problems, but the most serious was and still is accrediting training and the related issue of the 'training analysts.' In a surprising way the IPA's preoccupation with accreditation of training programs, the selection and vesting authority in training analysts, approving regional independency in accepting or rejecting theoretical modifications became the new cause of some new type of crises. The most common was blurring the boundaries between training and licensing the trainees to practice psychoanalysis. Psychoanalysts, everywhere, get the license to work with patients from their original academic education and training, which prepare them to do work with the public, not by the accredited training in an *IPA* institute. This point deserves a special attention.

Moving the attention from the subject matter of psychoanalysis to the issue of training resulted in gradual deterioration of the former, manifested in unexplainable splitting and the birth of school plurality, with no obvious or proven theoretical disagreements. Training gave the impression that the quality of the psychoanalysts will get better under the new more demanding programs. The result was disappointing as the publications in the main international journals have shown. Publication in clinical psychoanalysis was almost non-existent. Theoretical papers were mere elaboration of old more established works of analysts of time passed. It is natural that bad publications come from bad psychoanalysis not only bad analysts. Therefore, *we should put our efforts in improving psychoanalysis, not improving training of psychoanalysts.* Witnessing the deterioration of psychoanalysis, both as a profession and a theory should make us rethink this obstinate preoccupation with training instead of the subject matter of the problem, which is psychoanalysis.

The pioneers of psychoanalysis (apart from Freud) were not endowed theorists with very few exceptions who gave first and most interesting viewpoints of the subject (just to mention a few: Green, Matte-Bianco, Bion). They were also inclined to limit their explorations to the phenomena of psychopathology, and considered working on non-clinical issues mere application of psychoanalysis and a peripheral matter. The few who came from the humanities or literature were considered outsiders or made to feel that way. In spite of that, the theory of psychoanalysis as a theory of the subject flourished outside the psychoanalytic communities, especially in Europe. From the thirties of last century ordinary people showed great interest in everything human and attempted to examine, analyze, discover their hidden meaning. Ordinary people learned from psychoanalysis the duality of the manifest and the latent. They also accepted that the links in that duality are strange because of the unconscious processes. The term 'analyzing' pervaded all the idiographic scientific activities and had the same meaning it had in psychoanalysis. Movies, wars, social fads, political events, even the tendency to re-examining previous events in light of this new way of thinking took hold of the culture and the lives of the intellectuals everywhere. The psychoanalytical concept of the subject permeates the intellectual circles (but not psychoanalysis), and was used correctly and with success and enthusiasm. Since the beginning of twentieth century, there is a noticeable difference in the conception of the human subject and anything related to the *him*.

Psychoanalysis, the clinical and the non-clinical, is like the twins of *Hypnos* and *Thanatos*; one is waking up and the other is fading away. Psychoanalysis that is dying is clinical psychoanalysis; it is limited and unable to extend its theory to include the human subject as the subject matter of psychoanalysis. Tracing back the theory of psychoanalysis to its origin in dreams and the wish, passing by infantile sexuality and *Trieb*, then narcissism and the differentiations provided in the metapsychologies, and finally the official recognition of the subject as structural phenomenon; if we do that we will realize that psychoanalysis is a theory of the human subject and not of patients. This feature is unrecognized by clinicians because it is not part of the psychoanalysis they learn and train in the IPA institutes. Analysts and non-analyst have to respond to the idea that psychoanalysis is not a profession or a skill but a theory of subject.

Opinions about the subject based on presupposed judgments, (humans are such and such) are no longer accepted. Humans feel the obligation to sort out first the statements about their nature that were product of folklore, religions, preset statements of the old wise people, and getting factual ideas about themselves. This is not only a change in the attitude regarding 'us' but a change that considers the subject an objective for study. The other significant and recent change is a pervasive belief that understanding the subject, as an entity that has meaning to discover, is conditional on understanding all his human attributes because of their noticeable interdependencies and interrelationship.

Psychoanalysis has introduced to Western Culture, and incidentally globally, a very different human subject from the ones that were previously configured by other civilizations. It became clear that something different has to be done because of the drastic change psychoanalysis introduced to the stance from the subject. Psychoanalysis had to shed off the image of being just a psychotherapy technique. Human societies and human sciences are engaged in a process of reciprocating interaction. The change of the concept of the human subject – that is now an accepted idea – is not coincidental. Social and intellectual evolution is always determined by the previous changes in the society that caused the subject to change too. This is reason enough to look at psychoanalysis as one of the human sciences, not anything else or less. Adopting this kind of attitude is not easy and will happen differently in different sciences. It is expected to face resistance from psychoanalysts for reasons mentioned above, but most the resistance will come from psychoanalysts but for an unexpected reason: likely they do not know how to turn their profession into a science. Doing that requires knowledge that is not part of what they earn in training.

Psychoanalysis: Skill (Practice) or Science (Education)?

After Freud's discovery of psychoanalysis several idiographic sciences in the field of the humanities expanded to cover a wider range of the human phenomena. What psychoanalysis revealed of the intrapsychic core of the subject showed that any theory of the subject based on functional principles would fail in encompassing his true nature. But, the more impressive effect of *psychoanalysis was in being the first demonstrative structural approach to the study of the subject.* A concrete example is the theory of dreams. Although the book on dreams underlined the functional relation between the dream and the wish it also presented the structural nature of dreaming and its difference from waking-life thinking. The humanities adjusted to this fact and started to approach the subject structurally. Anthropology is a good illustration of a structural attitude toward social phenomena. Any comparison between the anthropology of Frazer's *The Golden Bough* (1894–2015), and Levi-Strauss's *Structural Anthropology* (1963) will reveal the contribution of psychoanalysis in changing anthropology from functionalism to structuralism. Structuralism – though was not yet conceived – appeared in every new intuition Freud had about the subject. It is hard to believe that Freud's impact on the Western Culture was result of functional insights and ignore the impact of his structural thought that peppered his whole of his text (changing the prevailing cause/effect links regarding homosexuality that were offered before psychoanalysis and suggesting a link between homosexuality and narcissism). Structuralism became the necessary background for any study and understanding of the subject. As such, the subject and the cultures he creates proved to contain a myriad of scientific potentials and endeavors that were not noticed before, and there are also interdependencies in the humanities in general that deny that psychoanalysis is just a skill of practice.

Psychoanalysis introduced to the humanities a psychologically living subject who is material for different approaches to understanding his diverse features. To develop this idea properly we have to overcome, or at least argue, objections that will possibly come from both the psychoanalysts and the scientists of the humanities, and may be also from the academicians. All the schools of psychoanalysis, despite their disagreements with the classical Freudian theory and the disagreements among themselves maintain that psychoanalysis is firstly part of the mental health professions, thus should be learned only in specialized training institutes. The idea that psychoanalysis belongs to the mental health profession kept being perpetuated blindly without any supporting evidence of its effectiveness or suitability to an advancing theory of the subject. Clinical psychoanalysts were not and still are not able to demonstrate and prove its effectiveness as psychotherapy. The results of psychotherapy are not verifiable in the traditions of research, as I will discuss a little later. The mandatory training in designated training institutes and limiting training to special professionals prevented capable and talented people from learning it because they were not mental health practitioners and were not interested in practicing psychotherapy. Psychoanalysis was snarled in its own trap. On the other side of the issue, the notion that psychoanalysis is more than a professional discipline did not sit well with the physicians and non-physicians who practice it as a profession. It is expected and understandable that the physicians, the clinical psychologists, and social workers would refuse to consider psychoanalysis more than psychotherapy. What attracted many not medical persons to train in psychoanalysis is the short cut it gives to the health profession.

This idea would divest it of the direct and indirect connection to the medical professions. The resistance to consider psychoanalysis a human science is rooted in two facts. In the last century or so, clinical psychoanalysts did not come up with anything new or of value to add to whatever is the range of the clinical sphere[1]. The new schools have nothing to contribute to the humanities. Human scientists have no interest in psychoanalysis especially that they have already developed their own method of using the structural method and have no need for input from the psychoanalysis of the training institutes. The second fact is the limited knowledge clinical analysts have of what the humanities are engaged in working on. The current system of training limits the clinical aspect of psychoanalysis to learn and assimilate some vital

---

[1] Following the early clinical literature and what was published in the last sixty years convinces the scientists of the humanities that psychoanalysis has nothing to offer them. However, there was a good period of time (the fifties and sixties of last centuries) when psychoanalysts along with thinkers and philosophers explored the nature of the human subject in a very rich and penetrating way, and applying psychoanalytic thinking in genuine creative ways. They were able to reveal the working of the unconscious in varied attributes of the subject ranging from theater and movies to politics and history. Some even tried their hand in very innovative techniques like Moreno in psychodrama (1987). Contemporary clinical psychoanalysis is far from being adequate to do something of that nature in the same fields.

knowledge available in other human sciences. For instance, psychoanalysts are in great need for knowledge that could come from the fields of child development, linguistics, the basis of cognitive failings, and the signs of affective improvement and maturity. Analysts, on the other hand are needed in the field of child psychology, socialization, and the dynamics of family interactions. Reciprocally, psychoanalytic knowledge is needed in the new fields of the effect of cultural fusions on identity and child rearing. They need to be part of the human sciences in that area because it will affect new concepts of psychopathology. Psychoanalysis has been and is in need of being involved in the research in those areas, although it would not yield itself to research.

With little exaggeration, we now have two types of psychoanalysts. Psychoanalysts who insist on limiting psychoanalysis to clinical work, implying that it has to remain a profession of psychotherapy, and should dedicate itself to training new comers. The other type does not care primarily about its place in the mental health field but prefers it to be part of the human sciences, which would have mutual interest in developing and improving the theory of the human subject. This is the minority.

The New Subject of Psychoanalysis

The way clinical psychoanalysis emerged and occupied the whole field of psychoanalysis reflects the basic fault in its evolution. A functional relationship between psychopathology and psychoanalytic findings got established early in the history of psychoanalysis. Freud and Breuer published, maybe, the first work on that subject (1895d). Freud continued to discover few novel things about hysteria, which were also discoveries in the splitting of consciousness. It was established in the late eighteen hundred that psychoanalysis' discoveries are in the field of the psychoneuroses, and its therapy. However, Freud, in a surprising way, published three major works within five years which were not clinical in any way; yet they were the foundation of a psychoanalytic movement. Freud's literature that followed his early functional understanding of psychopathology was none-clinical. Moreover, Freud's clinical work proved to be of poor quality to explain the reputation that psychoanalysis has gained. In the fifty years of his discoveries, insights, and intuitions which changed the field of the humanities beyond any expectations, only one of his clinical works – *The Wolf Man* – has some significance within the psychoanalytic community. On the other hand, most of those intuitions and discoveries had a tremendous effect on the discoveries of the human subject and contributed abundantly to the structural theories of the human subject. The Oedipus complex, narcissism, the workings of the primary process and the *Triebhaft* nature of human volition changed the subject from a mere epistemological entity to a dynamic epistemological duality. Freud's psychoanalysis changed the outlook of the subject, society, and most of the ideological beliefs regarding human nature. It took years – and mostly after Freud's death – for those discoveries to be applied clinically in a proper way, and by fewer numbers than expected.

When the field of psychiatric nosology was expanding – starting from the late forties – there were needs for clarifying and explaining the new and different categories of psychopathology. Differential diagnoses were very central in that process of expansion. Psychoanalysis attempted and successfully made psychopathology a field of discoveries and of giving differential diagnoses new meanings. There were even suggestions and quasi road maps for the psychotherapy of those psychopathologies (Fliess, 1950, 1970). However, the *IPA* kept training as the central issue in the psychoanalytic movement. This stance obstructed shifting the attention from exploring the subject further to restricting psychoanalysis to a practice of psychotherapy. Strangely, limiting psychoanalysis to an act of psychotherapy changed training itself. It went through the natural process, in situations like that, of getting more elaborate, complicated, and demanding for no practical reasons, but as the reason for keeping the IPA as the guardian of psychoanalysis.

The notion that training was done in improved institutes that are supervised and accredited by the International Organization turned the whole issue into a licensing process. This change had several serious problems, but the most serious was, and still is, accrediting training and the related issue of the "training analysts." In a surprising way the IPA's preoccupation with accreditation of training programs, the selection and vesting authority in training analysts, approving regional independency in accepting or rejecting theoretical modifications became the new cause of some new types of crises. The most common was blurring the boundaries between training and licensing the trainees to practice psychoanalysis. Psychoanalysts, everywhere, get the license to work with patients from their original academic education and training, which prepare them to do work with the public, not by the accredited training in an *IPA* institute. This point deserves a special attention.

Moving the attention from the subject matter of psychoanalysis to the issue of training resulted in gradual deterioration of the former, manifested in unexplainable splitting and the birth of school plurality, with no obvious or proven theoretical disagreements. Training gave the impression that the quality of the psychoanalysts will get better under the new more demanding programs. The result was disappointing as the publications in the main international journals have shown. Publication in clinical psychoanalysis was almost non-existent. Theoretical papers were mere elaboration of old more established works of analysts of time passed. It is natural that bad publications come from bad psychoanalysis not only bad analysts. Therefore, *we should put our efforts in improving psychoanalysis, not improving training of psychoanalysts.* Witnessing the deterioration of psychoanalysis, both as a profession and a theory should make us rethink this obstinate preoccupation with training instead of the subject matter of the problem, which is psychoanalysis.

The pioneers of psychoanalysis (apart from Freud) were not endowed theorists with very few exceptions who gave first and most interesting viewpoints of the subject (just to mention a few: Green, Matte-Bianco, Bionl). They were also inclined to limit their explorations to the phenomena of psychopathology, and considered working on non-clinical issues mere application of psychoanalysis and a peripheral matter. The few who came from the humanities or literature were considered outsiders or made to feel that way. In spite of that, the theory of psychoanalysis as a theory of the subject flourished outside the psychoanalytic communities, especially in Europe. From the thirties of last century ordinary people showed great interest in everything human and attempted to examine, analyze, and discover their hidden meaning. Ordinary people learned from psychoanalysis the duality of the manifest and the latent. They also accepted that the links in that duality are strange because of the unconscious processes. The term 'analyzing' pervaded all the idiographic scientific activities and had the same meaning it had in psychoanalysis. Movies, wars, social fads, political events, even the tendency to re-examine previous events in light of this new way of thinking took hold of the culture and the lives of the intellectuals everywhere. The psychoanalytical concept of the subject permeates the intellectual circles (but not psychoanalysis), and was used correctly and with success and enthusiasm.

Psychoanalysis, the clinical and the non-clinical, is like the twins of *Hypnos* and *Thanatos*; one is waking up and the other is fading away. Psychoanalysis that is dying is clinical psychoanalysis; it is limited and unable to extend its theory to include the human subject as the subject matter of psychoanalysis. Tracing back the theory of psychoanalysis to its origin in dreams and the wish, passing by infantile sexuality and *Trieb*, then narcissism and the differentiations provided in the metapsychologies, and finally the official recognition of the subject as structural phenomenon; if we do that, we will realize that psychoanalysis is a theory of the human subject and not of patients. This feature is unrecognized by clinicians because it is not part of the psychoanalysis they learn and train in the IPA institutes. Analysts and non-analysts have to respond to the idea that psychoanalysis is not a profession or a skill but a theory of subject.

Since the beginning of twentieth century there is a noticeable difference in the conception of the human subject and anything related to the *him*. Opinions about the subject based on presupposed judgments, (humans are such and such) are no longer accepted. Humans feel the obligation to sort out first the statements about their nature that were product of folklore, religions, preset statements of the old wise people, and getting factual ideas about themselves. This is not only a change in the attitude regarding 'us' but a change that considers the subject an objective for study. The other significant and recent change is a pervasive belief that understanding the subject as an entity that has meaning to discover is conditional on understanding all 'his' human attributes because of their noticeable interdependencies and interrelationships.

Psychoanalysis has introduced to Western Culture, and incidentally globally, a very different human subject from the ones that were previously configured by other civilizations. It became clear that something different has to be done because of the drastic change psychoanalysis introduced to the stance of the subject. Psychoanalysis had to shed off the image of being just a psychotherapy technique. Human societies and human sciences are engaged in a process of reciprocating interaction. The change of the concept of the human subject – that is now an accepted idea – is not coincidental. Social and intellectual evolution is always determined by the previous changes in the society that caused the subject to change too. This is reason enough to look at psychoanalysis as one of the human sciences, not anything else or less. Adopting this kind of attitude is not easy, and will happen differently in different sciences. It is expected to face resistance from psychoanalysts for reasons mentioned above, but most of the resistance will come from psychoanalysts but for an unexpected reason: it is likely they do not know how to turn their profession into a science. Doing that requires knowledge that is not part of what they earn in training.

Psychoanalysis as a Human Science

All sciences, in general terms, are specific unified body of facts gathered and checked for accuracy and truth in a systematic describable method. Their results are presented as laws of the subject matter of the science. Sciences are divided into two main categories: the category of physical matters (nomothetic sciences) and the category of the human subject (idiographic sciences). All sciences in each of the two main categories branch out into specialties, subspecialties, and overlap with neighboring sciences. Wundt's psychology of the end of last century and James's psychology of early in the twentieth century are now dozens of specialties with links to dozens of specialties in other fields. There are even areas of interest in both categories that invite connection between branches of the two main categories, like psychology and neurology.

Locating psychoanalysis in this system of classification requires starting with a fact. Psychoanalysis complements all the human sciences because considering the unconscious in any human phenomenon is essential to understanding it properly, and the human subject requires the psychoanalytic structural conception to reveal the core nature of his attributes. This fact is behind the change in the social fabric of Western societies and its culture. If psychoanalysis is just a method of psychotherapy, whatever its uniqueness and distinction could not have changed the Western culture the way psychoanalysis as human science did. Freud was very conscious of that when he said to Yung on their trip to the US (paraphrasing) that the Americans do not know what trouble they brought on themselves by inviting them. He was fully conscious that he was discovering more than psychotherapy. Whatever was discovered in the offices of psychoanalysts proved to be much more important than what the clinical conceptions envisaged and were more effective on a social level.

In the early chapters we have reviewed the history and the status of a psychoanalytic theory or a theory of psychoanalysis that could be firmly spelled out. All the attempt proved that such a firm identifiable theory does not exist. What exist, though, are several schools of thought regarding psychotherapy.

It is a paradox to have applications for a theory of psychoanalysis that is difficult for psychoanalysts to articulate. Only sciences[2], not their applications, have theories, thus, it is incumbent on us to prove that psychoanalysis is a science that has a theory, and its applications are set it up to become a component of the larger circle of sciences. Acknowledging that psychoanalysis is a science and not just a practice of psychotherapy should be a major shift in the attitude toward advancing clinical psychoanalysis itself. It requires that clinical psychoanalysis would not be considered the psychoanalytic knowledge, or that developing, improving, and modernizing psychoanalysis should be restricted to clinical discoveries. Making that shift will advance the quality of the theoretical basis of clinical psychoanalysis and offers the new

---

[2] It should be mentioned here that the analyst was also more silent than silent. Although that moment of transference interaction was available for some sort of mentioning to the patient, I thought it is better to just let transference shape the rest of the analytic scene.

generations of psychoanalytic practitioners, and psychoanalytic intellectuals a wider perspective of the subject.

It is also necessary to consider psychoanalysis a human science because limiting it to a mental health specialty distances it from any other source of useful knowledge like psychology and psychiatry. Psychoanalysis is fundamentally based on the duality of conscious-unconscious, which it shares with all other human science. Psychoanalysis is also rich with insights regarding the psychopathological meaning of symptoms. It has something to offer the humanities, and something to offer psychiatry, especially in the field of diagnoses and differential diagnosis. Acknowledging that psychoanalysis is a human science requires from the psychoanalysts to realize that psychoanalysis is going to branch out into specialties that links with other sciences, not necessarily only idiographic ones[3]. Lately, psychoanalysts are showing genuine interest in neurology, as neurology is similarly speculating about some psychoanalytic concepts. The budding interest of psychoanalysts in neurology has some features of fakeness or superficiality, because the discussions about that link is concentrating on the hope that neurology could provide physical evidence that is needed to validate the psychoanalytic theory. It is self-interest, not a genuine interest in neurology itself. This fakeness shows itself more clearly in making no mention or giving any consideration to how that link should affect and changes training of psychoanalysts.

Moreover, psychoanalysts are eagerly looking for research that could support the reliability of psychoanalytic findings and the outcome of the process of treatment. There is belief that proving that psychoanalysis works (by some research), would be the solution to the drop of interest in it. This is a false premise. When psychoanalysis was still not yet a full-fledged theory or profession, and was grappling with identifying its technique which was giving tentative poor results, it still created great interest and reached its peak of popularity without any research to support its claims. Psychoanalysis was promising a theory of the subject, which was of great importance in the late nineteen hundredth. People were seeing what psychoanalysis was coming up with, which was what made sense to what was merely insensible before. No research was needed to prove the credibility of its revelations because its theoretical output was convincing as is. Psychoanalysis surpassed the threshold of being a nomothetic science from the beginning, and it independently gained

---

[3] It should be mentioned here that the analyst was also more silent than silent. Although that moment of transference interaction was available for some sort of mentioning to the patient, I thought it is better to just let transference shape the rest of the analytic scene.

the credibility needed without any evidence of being an effective psychotherapy.

There is a point that could be missed in the fact that psychoanalysis gained credibility without any proof of its validity. The recent attempts of the schools of psychoanalysis to shift the focus from the intrapsychic to issues of relatedness caused psychoanalysis to lose its particular subject matter. Relatedness is the subject matter of half a dozen other human sciences. *The intrapsychic is the subject matter of psychoanalysis alone.* Psychoanalysis lost its credibility and status because it lost its identity and became an appendage to the idiographic filed of research without proof that it belongs there. For instance, psychoanalysis of the intrapsychic led to acknowledging the important effect of the interfamilial dynamics on the formation of the intrapsychic in the child. The field of the psychological life of the child opened the door to thinking about rearing techniques and education. Piaget's structural psychology was a veritable child psychology that replaced Gesell's[4] child psychology of the beginning of last century. It was natural that the findings in that field would attract the attention to the processes of socialization and social interaction. This last point created a boom of research in most of the areas that psychology had a role in rejuvenating, like group psychology and social conflict. Those fields – that became branches of the humanities – are extensions of psychoanalysis as a theory of the subject and an intrapsychic entity.

Scientists do systematic observations and explorations and examine the data they gather by acknowledged and stated methods. They present their findings in a form of principles or laws. Other scientists who could check the methodology of the research, knowing the details of the research would verify the correctness of those results. *Does psychoanalysis qualify as a science of that nature?* The immediate answer is that psychoanalysis – in its present condition – does not qualify as a science. Nonetheless, psychoanalysis opened four principle areas of explorations that qualify it to join the humanities as one of its branches. I name them in the sequence they historically appeared in the history of the psychoanalytic movement, and linked with each other to change the general concept of the subject:

The *first* is the psychosexual prototype of the subject's development from infancy to maturity. The inclusion of infantile sexuality in the psychology of

---

[4] It should be mentioned here that the analyst was also more silent than silent. Although that moment of transference interaction was available for some sort of mentioning to the patient, I thought it is better to just let transference shape the rest of the analytic scene.

the subject made development and evolution a basic idea in any thought of the subject. Before the discovery of psychoanalysis, it did not occur to scientists to think of psychical phenomena as having a preliminary status in childhood and follow a schema of progression and evolution.

The *second* is the subjective and personalized links engendered by the intrapsychic that links his different dualities to each other. This notion revealed the basis of the uniqueness of the psyche. It became a basic feature in the humanities to think and search for the processes behind the personal psychological scenes that are involved in the formation of the rest of psychological phenomena. It was the psychoanalytic contribution to structuralism.

The *third* is accepting that in all psychical phenomena are the product of fusion of the thesis and antithesis of in the subject's duality and not simple ontological entities. This feature is essential to keep in mind that whatever the phenomenon is it has a latent meaning that we could be reach if it is analyzed[5].

The *forth* is the continuity of early experiences and their everlasting influence in later experiences. Psychoanalysis, both clinically and as part of the humanities revealed the double inscription of the unconscious in consciousness, thus there is constant transference of past to present.

The four areas defined above are fields of explorations; we know very little about, and without exploring them scientifically psychoanalysis will continue in the same direction: deteriorating and shrinking. In addition, those four fields of explorations could be approached in the manner that would revolutionize research in the science of the subject. They could also be source of great research hypotheses. Those researches are not to validate psychoanalysis but to expand it.

Psychoanalysis and Research

Research is the prerequisite for any issue considered scientifically proven. It is the way the scientist makes sure and be sure that what he is talking about is valid because he could repeat what he did or does and get the same result. His conclusions could also be tested by others and confirm their validity of his finding. A science is the product of the researches that accumulated its body of knowledge. Sciences are divided into two main groups: nomothetic and

---

[5] It should be mentioned here that the analyst was also more silent than silent. Although that moment of transference interaction was available for some sort of mentioning to the patient, I thought it is better to just let transference shape the rest of the analytic scene.

idiographic. Nomothetic sciences pertain to the physical world and search for the causes of the physical events, because the physical events do not disclose their causes spontaneously. Nomothetic sciences are fundamentally deductive sciences and produce functional theories. They also share the experimental model in examining the physical phenomena because it is possible to control the subject of the research.

The other group is the idiographic sciences, which pertains to the human phenomena. Human phenomena are too multifaceted to deduce from it what could explain them. Therefore, human sciences aim at getting the *meaning* of the phenomena inductively. The aim of the idiographic sciences is getting theories of the structural nature of the phenomena. The experimental model is not possible in the idiographic because the human phenomena are not pliant to the demands of exact comparisons. It is impossible to do scientific research in psychoanalysis as it stands now, because of the complexity of the issues that could be raised for research: like its therapeutic effectiveness.

However, psychoanalysts could turn some of their clinical observation into research issues if they were trained and exposed to a scientific milieu. An example of what I mean by turning a clinical observation into a scientific issue relates what analysts notice in the reaction of patients who have or lack of a sense of humor to interpretations. The patients who have a sense of humor are more responsive to interpretations and more cooperative in the process of reconstruction than the ones who lack in those two domains. Interpretations and reconstruction include and embarrass ironies that are basic in humor. A question, or maybe several questions arise from a general theory of epistemology regarding humor. Then, if the analyst has a background in child psychology he might seek his child psychology colleague's help in knowing how and when do children respond to ironies and what constitute an irony in their development. Taking this research result back to training and the practice of psychoanalysis the analyst will be smarter in configuring his interpretations. The research could be extended to cover people (or patients) who have poor sense of humor and if that is a psychodynamic deficiency or a pathological condition.

This 'issue' has three elements: sense of humor, psychodynamic deficiency (childhood deprivation), and psychopathology. Each of those elements could be observed and 'examined' separately by psychologists, clinical psychoanalysts, sociologists, or social workers. However, to give it the status of a scientific research it is important to define what is going to be precisely observed (which needs a psychologist to develop the psychometric measures for that precision), a method to tabulate the patients' verbal content, and a statistical design to translate the tabulated verbal content. In other words, research in psychoanalysis could begin with a hypothesis derived from psychoanalytic observation and the rest of the reach will need the expertise of research specialists. Lately the role of the statistician has become of great importance in the planning of research. Accordingly, the clinical psychoanalyst needs the expertise of the statistician to formulate the hypotheses of his research so that the statistician could decide how the results should be tabulated in a way that makes possible for the results to be quantifiable.

Research in psychoanalysis is a research effort of more than the psychoanalyst; it is a collaborative work of several skills. This picture of the relationship of research to psychoanalysis is convincing that psychoanalysis belongs to academia. Firstly, the knowledge in the field of psychoanalysis has expanded to an extent that makes it impossible to learn it in the same institute setup that was established fifty or sixty years ago. The discoveries about the subject outside clinical psychoanalysis are very much needed in clinical psychoanalysis and should be part of training. A clinical psychoanalyst has to know more about the human subject and his life involvements than learning about the different technique of doing therapy in the different schools. At the same time, the input from psychoanalysis to make more sense to the other human sciences requires clinical psychoanalysis to learn the language of the other human sciences. The link between psychoanalysis and the rest of the human sciences is not matter of convenience; it is a matter of necessity. We are now more sophisticated in our views about psychoanalytic therapy, and we have more complex issues to examine. All that cannot be done by psychoanalysts who are trained in the limited milieu of the training institutes. Letting go of our familiar and endeared psychoanalytic history is a must to accept moving psychoanalysis to academia.

Chapter Eleven
Psychoanalyzing and Psychotherapy

The previous chapter could be difficult for contemporary clinical psychoanalysts to follow and assimilate, or appreciate. For few decades, since the seventies of the last century, the ideas and the vocabulary of the classical theory are not used in the literature anymore. Moreover, training programs in the institutes are not geared toward teaching basic theory. They are tending more to teach the popular contemporary thought and the works of the most popular analysts. The notion that training in practice has enough theory allows reducing the time for the basic classical theory. If we add to that the new school with each having its theory, we can understand the difficulty that contemporary psychoanalysts have with a classical examination of the concept of the subject. However, I believe there are many psychoanalysts who are disappointed and disillusioned in the results of their training, and are eager to practice psychoanalysis the proper way within a solid theory of psychoanalysis.

Most of the arguing about training is naturally going to be centered on the tripartite system of personal analysis, supervision, and the seminars. Personal analysis was originally suggested as a didactic phase. It changed to become for therapeutic purposes; so learning how analysis is done is no longer essential in training. Supervision seems to be related more to clinical practice than to theoretical implication. Although some supervisors have the chance to discuss few theoretical issues that pertain to practice, it is not common that supervision would take account of theoretical explanations because supervisors try to avoid conflicts with the other supervisors who might be of different in their orientations. Fifty years ago, it was common that the seminars were not just for teaching the basics of the theory; very thought-provoking reviews of the basics were common material the training faculty included in the regular presentation. Discussing the classical theory was a serious consideration because it was used to show the 'psychoanalytic way of thinking.' I am aware and I also suspect that the part of the seminars dedicated to the classical theory has shrunk because teaching the classical theory is of no value if it is not done scholarly. The classical theory has the history of discovering the subject, i.e., the raison d'être of the birth of psychoanalysis. Therefore, learning it well and in a scholarly manner was, and should still be, a serious endeavor.

The most obvious feature of bypassing the classical theory is evident in the contemporary literature of psychoanalysis. The trend to explain classical concepts in some doubtful and unsupported new theoretical formulation was popular in in the eighties of the last century (Compton, 1981, Simon, 1981). Currently the trend is presumably updating or correcting old traditional concepts by explaining them by meaning derived from the recent theoretical suggestions (Natterson & Friedman, 1995). A second complication in the link between training and learning is the "training analysts." This topic occupied a large space in the literature in the last two decades, without coming to a satisfying conclusion. Analysis – as it was originally initiated – was a skill that could be learned the way trades were learned in the middle ages: a master tradesman transmitting his knowledge and experience directly from a generation to the next. From the beginning psychoanalytic formation was entrusted to senior analysts. For five decades the system worked. Training issues emerged only with the emergence of the schools and the senior analysts who became training analysts got involved in the new versions of psychoanalysis and the trend of theoretical plurality. The training analysts of the age of the school emphasized their clinical distinction over their theoretical knowledge, and not teaching or supervising anything that does not pertain to their particular practice. There is a third problem in that regard. Psychoanalysis could be taken both as a transitive verb and as a noun: as a verb it is an act that requires *training*, but as a noun it is a body of knowledge that demands *learning*. Although psychoanalysts are likely to deny that, thinkers and scientist of the humanities have no difficulty acknowledging this fact. We can manage the spontaneous rejection of the fundamentals of the classical theory by discussing 'psychoanalyzing' in terms of clinical practice, thus we stay in the comfortable zone of the contemporary psychoanalyst.

Intrapsychic – The act of psychoanalyzing could be summarized as an act of discovering the subject within the patient, which means finding out with the patient the influences that built and created his intrapsychic. In doing so, the patient reviews his life experiences with the analyst since his childhood, and the analyst interprets the manner they shaped his psychological make-up. However, there is the person who seeks therapy because of suffering from his intrapsychic pressures, which he cannot understand to be able to manage. Another, could be suffering from the inability to control the intrapsychic pressures that affects his relationships with others. The therapist should be careful and considerate of the stance he will take in psychotherapy with either of them. The significance of this point is whether the therapist is going to do psychoanalysis, or resort to therapeutic techniques that could just 'help' the patient. Making that choice has to be decided by proper assessment of the patient's attitudes, aspirations, and his ability to deal with the therapeutic process. The assessment should investigate the patient's capability of gaining insight in discovering 'unconsciousness.'

Another consideration has to be given to the patient's ability to bear the restrictions psychoanalysis requires in order to be done properly (the clinical protocol). There are patients who could tolerate the boundaries of the tripartite protocol, while others prefer a regular relationship with the therapist and developing unrestricted relationship with him. *A clinical assessment of that aspect should be guided by the patient's state, not by the therapist's preference of the approach he takes.* It was surprising to me to realize with time and with the deterioration of psychoanalysis that psychoanalysts also differ in their preferences, not only the patients. What is important is not what the analyst prefers but what is better for the patient.

The Essentials of Psychoanalyzing

The basic theoretical premise of the classical theory is that the subject's intrapsychic dynamics, which is always a structure of dualities, is typified by unconscious links between the duos in those dualities. The work of interpretation is the only means to dealing with those links. Therefore, psychoanalyzing is the method of revealing the unconscious links within the dualities of the patient's intrapsychic conflicts. In a case of phobia of heights, working on the patient's trend to impulsively take the wrong decision in his daily life, revealed to the patient and the analyst that his phobia was related to that fear of compulsively taking the wrong decision and jump. Making the unconscious links in the duo of 'do or not do' it was possible put the phobia within the patient's character formation.

The three conditions of the Freudian protocol ought to mean to the analysts to refrain from developing a relationship with the patient beyond or different from the boundaries of the therapeutic one, and to work mainly on transference material i.e., the psychoanalyst should not assume a role like kindness, understanding, wisdom, or even 'the one who knows' in doing analysis. The analyst is not supposed to give opinions or share one with the patient in regards to matters that are of personal nature. Not doing that would change the professional relationship to many other things beyond the patient or the analyst to know. In addition to anonymity and neutrality the analyst abstains from satisfying or frustrating requests by the patient because neither he nor the patient knows the unconscious demand in the request. Those three conditions, in addition to free association and interpretation are in accord with the notion that psychoanalysis is treating intrapsychic difficulties, not interpersonal matters.

The psychoanalytic relationship, or the protocol of the analytic situation has to be introduced and explained to the patient before starting the analysis, because it could be frustrating and misunderstood and maybe also become hurting, if it is not stipulated and explained earlier before the analysis starts. This stance is not only rejected by the *relationist* analysts, it is even denounced and judged negatively by the intersubjective school of analysis. Renick (1993) postulated that "everything an analyst does in the analytic situation is based upon his or her personal psychology. This *limitation* (italics added) cannot be reduced let alone done away with; we have only to admit it or denying it." Classical analysts are aware of that fact (they are the first to conceive and reveal it), but in their practice, they do what all ordinary people are capable of doing in their daily relationships with others: restrain themselves from forcing their own psychology on the patients. Moreover, analysts are presumed to be less neurotic than the average and 'trained' to check their reactions more rigorously and better than their patients. It is rather amateurish to think of one's unconscious as a thing that the analyst is helpless in confronting. We should also keep clear – in the analyst's mind – that interpretation deals with 'material' delivered by the patient (not according to a theoretical line of a school), and its interpretation has to come only from within the material itself. Therefore, if the analyst knows psychoanalysis well, the psychology of the analysts would not infiltrate the act of interpretation. Keeping the patient's material apart from theoretical leanings of the analyst and referring them to their origin in transference manifestations dictates what the analyst will respond to and what the interpretation will be about.

Renick (1995), continued justifying doing away with the parameters of interpretation by saying: "The major difficulty with the technical injunction against self-disclosure is that anonymity for the analyst is impossible – not only complete anonymity, any anonymity at all (468)." If that is the case, what does personal analysis and training do to prepare a candidate to what to do and not to do in practice? Renick's (1993, 1995, 1996, 1998, 2007), and most intersubjective analysts (Storolow, et al, 2001), confuse anonymity with self-disclosure. The clinical vignettes they provided are all regarding self-disclosure of their endeavors to explain who they are. They implicitly suggest that being anonymous is as if keeping from the patient some personal affairs. This obsession with self-disclosure reached the level of considering it part of the therapeutic work of the analyst. There are many negative things to be said about the detrimental effect of such exposure to the process of 'therapy' itself. Just as one obvious drawback is the patient's apprehensiveness to tailor his associations to fit the analyst's declared preferences. Self-disclosure is a recipe for turning psychoanalysis into a *folie à deaux*, and chaos of mutual loss of boundaries, which is the elementary principle in establishing a therapeutic setting. Boundaries are also the essence of any 'healthy' human encounter. A vignette could highlight more aspects of psychoanalyzing in contrast to psychotherapy

A patient was in analysis for more than a year. He came to his session, laid down on the couch, sighed, and was silent for few minutes. Then, he said that he was about to fall asleep. I responded by saying: and be more silent than silent. The patient turned his head to look at me and said with a smile: how could someone be more silent than silent? I had in mind that while he was silent, he had things going through his mind and that he was not silent; he just did not talk. I did not disclose that idea to him and kept the door open for his view of what was happening during his silence. As he did not expect an answer from me (I will discuss later the specifics of the psychoanalytic situation) he kept silent for few more moments then said: "My father was more silent than silent, especially after we lost my mother. I used to go to my room and cry for his loss, not mine"[1]. He continued by recalling memories of his father – 'a man of few words' – his relationship with his wife, more preconscious ideas and feelings regarding the home atmosphere, and the sense of his father's loneliness and its impact on the family. Not responding to the patient's request and not disclosing the analyst's own thoughts is a precondition for psychoanalyzing. The patient early mentioning of 'was going to fall asleep' was not clear in meaning but found its relevance later in the session.

There are two points worthy of being underlined regarding that moment. The first is the emergence of the unconscious in the conscious material of the transference. There were two silent people in that scene: the analyst and the patient. Although the analyst knew that something must be going on in the patient's mind, he did not ask him to report them. Instead, the analyst gave the patient all the space in the session and refrained from taking any part of it by initiating a relationship around silence. The result was the emergence of a third silent person in the scene, and the session changed to be a window to some memories of intrapsychic dynamics, and preconscious material relating to

---

[1] It should be mentioned here that the analyst was also more silent than silent. Although that moment of transference interaction was available for some sort of mentioning to the patient, I thought it is better to just let transference shape the rest of the analytic scene.

silence. The preconscious material led to memories of affective nature that were significant at a later time in the analysis. Many of them were related to boredom and guilt. In psychoanalyzing, the emergence of the unconscious does not happen as a discovery or uncovering something hidden. The unconscious is always there in the link between the manifest and the latent, in the duo that is gripping the patient's conflict, and most of all in the choice of words chosen by the patient to expresses himself. If that process is not interrupted by responding and relating to the patient as a person, and not his associations, the patient's words will reveal the unconscious link between what he says and what is latent in what he says.

Interpretation and Reconstruction

The duality of conscious-unconscious, and the duality of subject-object are commonly accepted by analyst of any school. Psychoanalysis played and still plays a major role in creating the bridge that links the duos in those dualities through resolving the linguistic issue that separate them. It was specified (see Chapter Three) that the counterpart talks the language of the primary processes, while the subject speaks only secondary process language. Freud called the process of working on the two languages 'translation'[3] (1896 b), yet he also called it interpretation. There is an important difference in the meaning of the two terms. In translation we do not expect, or are expected to add something to the original text. In interpretation, we listen to deduce from what we hear hidden meanings (unconscious), which becomes a new text. In psychoanalysis, we practice 'interpretation' and not of translation, because we read the patient's psychopathological text and note that it is not the exact statements that he would have liked to say. The subject is an entity that is not to be taken as it presents itself; it has to be interpreted even when is seems to be completely understandable.

Laplanche & Pontalis said: "Interpretation is the heart of the Freudian doctrine and technique" (1973, p. 227). Practicing psychoanalysis endeavor to make the conscious rhetoric tell us more than what the subject speech is saying. This phrase could also be formulated as establishing a way for the I (conscious) to communicate with *me* (unconsciousness) so we hear them both talking about the same thing in two different speeches.

Nasio (1984) said, "If we want to sum up the analyst's comportment, we may say: silence is the norm, explanatory interventions are frequent, and interpretations are rare" (p. 403). I would add to this succinct statement a small point of elucidation; analyst strives to also give meaning to the act of interpretation itself. The patient usually expects the analyst to explain not just

161

interpret what he says. The analyst should make clear from the beginning and all through the analysis that interpretation is what the patient has to look into to discover the explanations he seeks in therapy. Most of the patient's speech is an intricate system of subjective explanations, which are rarely right. But even when they are right, they are incomplete and missing their unconscious origin. The analyst's silence in response to the patient's effort to explain his own understanding is the way to prevent the patient's explanations from becoming statements of circumstance or fact. The analyst is supposed to interpret not explain to avoid making the act of analyzing become a situation that encourages regression and dependency on the analyst. Without that abstention the analysts would lead the patient to belief that the analyst's explanations are interpretations (Freud's recommendation of the principle of abstinence). The analyst's silence is a passive segment of an interpretation (you did not say everything about that issue yet).

At this point we get to address the link between meaning and cause in psychoanalysis, because interpretations are sometimes received by the patient as discoveries of the causes and not just the meanings that were implicit in his speech. Among the other things the analyst clarifies to the patient about the process of psychoanalyzing, which is the difference between interpretations and the meanings to speculate and causes to consider. The analyst should underline to the patient from the beginning that difference clearly but subtly). If the analyst is not careful in the way he formulates his interpretation it will not convey a sense of explaining to the patient, and the patient might take the analyst's words as interpretation. An explanation brings out a cause which will substitute a conscious element with another conscious element. Interpretation, on the hand, is the meaning that was unconsciously entwined in the conscious rhetoric.

A clinical vignette could explain the difference. A patient complained and explained his father's persistent demand of him to do better as an expression of dissatisfaction and thinking of his son as lacking the will to do his best. After a rather long stretch of analysis the patient thought that maybe the analyst's comments (interpretations) on those memories meant the opposite: his father expected him to do better because he thought well of him. After he noticed the apparent change in his perception of his father's view of him a chain of new memories followed of his father's own frustrated ambitions. The patient realized that he was to his father both the success he did not achieve and the pain of his failure. The patient came with opposite explanations for both his father's intentions and his difficulty in appeasing his father's anxiety. As the analyst refrained from explaining anything but just interpreted the patient's impasse as dealing with two possible opposing reasons for his father's attitude, and his own ambivalent image of the father, some analytic work was done. The patient became conscious of being – to the father – a representation of his own fears and frustrations, and that he unconsciously remained identifying with his father's preoccupation with success and failure. The interpretation put his freedom to choose what to do with inheriting his father's problem in a perspective of cure.

Interpreting the patient's associations is the essential work of the analyst, but it is just a means to an end. It is a means to making the story line of the patient's life less fragmented and confusing, with less gaps in its timeline, organized enough to spontaneously integrate new findings in the continuing psychoanalytic process, and eventually for the analytic work to continue after the termination of analysis. The changed features during an analysis are based on the interpretations given, but require another essential piece of work. The analyst has to help the patient *construct* his interpreted living experience in a lifeline to put some order in his expanding and new sense of being. Freud said about construction: "I think that construction is by far the more appropriate description [of the psychoanalytic technique]. Interpretation applies to something that one does to some single element of the material, such as an association or parapraxis. But it is construction when one lays before the subject of the analysis a piece of his early history that he has forgotten" (1937b, 261). Freud's statement emphasizes the idea that the subject – the patient in particular – needs to get stability and continuity to his fragmented life story, because of the unconscious sections of his life. There is a subtle but important clarification to make at this juncture.

Interpretation restores the meaning to a psychical event that seems to be missing in its manifest content, or clarifies the confusion about the psychodynamics of a certain process. It also deals – more or less – with the discovered meaning if the patient understands interpretations as an explanation of a causative aspects in some of the material the delivers. Construction, on the other hand, creates dynamics of its own that is independent of the dynamics of the setup of explanations that has been given by the patient to his psychological life. Furthermore, an interpretation could lead to explaining something that is of unclear causal nature, which was preconscious, thus turns unclarity into consciousness. In the Dora Case (Freud, 1905 e), the interpretation of the first dream brought about the preconscious understanding of the dynamics of the relationship of the father, Her K, and Frau K, and her position in that relationship. But in the Case of Katharina (Freud 1895, d) interpreting the somatic symptoms reconstructed the childhood sexual abuse scene. Thus, there is a difference between interpretations that 'explain' things, and interpretations that reconstruct the links between things.

Laplanche (1992) elaborated this point by saying: "Interpretation...finds itself trapped in the unresolvable dualism of pure factuality on the one hand [the genetic] and creative imagination on the other: in the one case, it patiently reconstitutes facts which it hopes will prove to be the source of determinism, explaining the present by the past" (p. 441). We encounter that kind of work in reconstruction when the two types of interpretations are enveloped in one meaningful narrative. It has to be emphasized that a psychoanalytic interpretation is not the simple act (or even a complex act) of attributing a set of associations (signifieds) to another set (signifiers). It is not even a process of referring the present to a certain past. It is the act of making meaning that becomes more than just an addition to the rhetoric of the patient.

Without a clear understanding of the way interpretation works, neither the manifest (the repressed and preconscious) which we try to explain, nor the latent (the past and unconscious) which we try to uncover, would be enough to give us a hint to the relationship between them. The relationship between the preconscious and the unconscious is essential for conceptualizing either if not both. Ricoeur (1970) defined the place of interpretation in psychoanalysis this way: "the problem of interpretation is coextensive with the problem of meaning or representation. Thence, psychoanalysis is interpretative from beginning to end" (p. 66). Waelder, after identifying transference as a special case of the compulsion to repeat, put those two points of view together in one comprehensive statement. He said (1987): "One cannot possibly talk about the handling of transference without talking also about interpretation; and one cannot talk about resistance either, without taking in consideration the interpretation of, and the use of interpretation against resistance" (p. 49).

It is the right place in our exposition to bring to focus the fact that the subject is an entity that has no one steady meaning, but an entity that exists only in the interpretations it evokes and the reconstruction it points toward. Nevertheless, the psychoanalysts, who were and are tempted to have their own theories, refuse this fact and try to bypass it. They still treat the subject as an ontological entity that is identifiable and definable, and that psychopathology is conditions created by events that caused it. In their work they even create terminologies that suit their explanations, and give their schools the names of what they call their relationship with their patients.

The second point is the nature of the unconscious in the work of psychoanalyzing. The unconscious is the adjective of the process that disguises unprocessed psychical issues and allows them to remain in consciousness though unnoticed or unrecognizable by the other, including the psychoanalyst. This point is well summarized in what Nasio was quoted above (1984) regarding silence, explanation, and interpretation. Silence is the analyst's response to the absence of unconscious material in the association. Explanations are assigning a meaning to some preconscious material (not only verbal). Silence conveys the sense of incompleteness. Interpretations are not reconstruction of explanations but are the main material for reconstruction.

In psychoanalysis, as practiced in the way mentioned above, the unconscious appears in the fabric of consciousness and not as a separate material thing. Psychoanalyzing separates it from its entanglements in the issue of consciousness. Thus, it will always appear in preconscious material that requires rephrasing and retelling to attain the format of the secondary process. In the case of the patient mentioned above the silent father was a reference to some painful family events which were non-verbal, and when they came back in analysis and the patient gave them some verbal connotations analysis was heading toward rumination.

The Freudian Clinical Protocol in Perspective

The anonymity in Renick's thinking discounts the role of countertransference. The issue of countertransference does not resolve by self-disclosure. On the contrary, self-disclosure does not add anything to psychoanalyzing except the analyst's need to show the patient something of himself. This point deserves serious discussions because it could be missed and psychoanalysis becomes more than a job the analyst is paid to do but becomes an arena for exhibitionism. Renick and the intersubjective analysts consider their approach to therapy 'democratization,' yet the patient, and the patient alone, has to have the whole psychoanalytic scene for himself and not be shared with the analyst in a democratic[2] gesture. This is in addition to the fallacy of a patient who is supposed to reveal everything about himself, and an analyst who reveals his thoughts about the analysis and maybe himself too.

Intersubjective analyst's criticism of anonymity in Freud's protocol is based on misunderstanding its meaning in analysis. Anonymity is preserved and remains valid as long as the analyst does not confirm or deny what the patient thinks or knows of him, or made himself believe about the analyst. The meaning of the term is in the purpose of practicing it: giving the patient the space and liberty to define the analyst as his psychology dictates, without the

---

[2] The political usage of the term democracy to describe the relationship with the analyst is a serious distortion of both the meaning of the term and the nature of psychoanalysis as a profession. The function of the analyst as the one who learned his profession and is practicing distinguishes him from the patient; who eventually has to pay the analyst for his work.

interference of the analyst so-called reality, or the feeling that he is secretly hiding unacceptable views about the analyst. The patient is left to himself to form his opinion of the analysts, whether it comes from actual information, rumors, and impressions of others or of his own. All that is not enough to create a relationship with the analyst, and all those ideas about the analyst will come up in the transference relationship, whatever the analyst tries to do to obviate that outcome. Moreover, the analyst's abstention of confirming or denying the patient's views of him prevents foreclosing on the unconscious elements in the analytic relationship of both the patient and the analyst. If the patient knew concrete facts about the analyst and disclosed them asking or observing the analyst's reaction, the analyst's refraining from confirming or denying any of it would turn the matter into a revival of old common curiosity of the child about his parent's private life. *Knowing about the analyst, but not from him, still brings about the unconscious side of the curiosity.*

In light of what is published nowadays in clinical work, neutrality is considered as human relation with the patient, not a clinical condition. It is judged as detachment, distance, lack of empathy, and most of all 'artificial and unrealistic.' It could be all of that if the analyst believed that he – as the analyst – is the tool and agent of cure, and the act of psychoanalyzing the intrapsychic complexities is an extra duty that he only ought to attend to. The analyst is the person who administers the act of cure, which is psychoanalysis, and he should assume that his cures come from psychoanalysis – practiced well – and that he is just a curing agent.

The second item in the Freudian protocol is Neutrality, or refraining from responding positively or negatively to the patient's demands for satisfying his wishes (within the range of physical sensibility). Neutrality is essential in psychoanalysis because it gives insights into the patient's infantile experiences of helplessness and its role in the formation of intrapsychic. It is also of the same importance to the relationist psychoanalyst because it reveals the patient's sense of entitlement, expectations, reactions to frustrations; etc. It is a stand the analyst takes from a major aspect of transference. A neutral analyst could discover to the patient those unconscious childhood structures, and uses that in reconstructing a great part of his past. Neutrality is also the indicator of analyst's own awareness of his narcissistic temptations to respond to some of the patients' demand to get the patient's reactions. In some of the vignettes that are sometimes published about clinical work, the analyst falls in the trap of the patient's transference-resistance and gives that resistance social and moral meanings, to avoid interpreting it as transference. This is a common mistake in the practice of new candidates. But I noticed in supervising already trained analysts (not candidates) that refraining from giving interpretations to the patient's demands was usually to avoid negative responses which the experienced analyst can anticipate its outcome. The patient should not be protected from the frustrations of neutrality.

Abstinence is best expressed by a recommendation from Winnicott. He strongly advised the psychoanalyst to avoid asking the patient questions 'because all what he will get from the patient is answers.' Analysts do not seek information; they seek the psychological importance of the information. Asking questions fulfils the patient's wish to know more about the analyst by either guessing what the analyst is interested in, or by playing with the answer to know that. Thus, abstinence is a way of avoiding foreclosure on the process of free association. The analyst should not give his parameters, which is not only better to keep from the patient as a point of guessing, but also to limit the analyst's unconscious laziness by keeping him alert to what could come as new and revealing material. This attitude, like the attitude of anonymity, makes the analyst uncommitted to the patient's desire to know where the analyst stands in regard to his associations.

The Conditions of Psychoanalyzing

The material psychoanalysts get from their patients, whether as associations or reactions to the work done, does not come from real and actual relationships with others or even the analyst himself. They are always fusion of several sources of the patients' rhetoric. The analyst better take the position that the patient is unconscious of mixing the past with the present, even when he talks about each separately. That theoretical principle makes the analyst limits his work to the transference of old and infantile experiences that shows in the therapeutic relationship. Therefore, psychoanalysis has to be practiced within a clear and defined setup (the analytic situation) in which boundaries between the analyst and the patient are clearly marked. They will be broken by the patient but when that happens (and it always happens) it will then be possible to show the patients their transferential nature. Those boundaries are Freud's clinical protocol. The reaction of the patient to those restrictions will also be part of the phenomenon of transference.

The rest of the psychoanalytic conditions, which will be mentioned a little later, should also be articulated, explained, given the reason behind them, and emphasized as part of the therapeutic work. The importance of limiting the patient's psychoanalytic experience to the phenomenon of transference[3] is not possible without working within the tripartite aspects of Freud's protocol, and the three basic dualities, discussed in chapter eight. To explain that correctly we should underline the difference between the classical point of view of transference and the relational psychotherapies' dealings with analytical material. Psychoanalysts limit the analytic work to the one relationship of subject/patient. This relationship is one directional: from the patient to the analyst. Therefore, for psychoanalyzing to happen the analyst has to 'freeze' his subjectivity (this is what training is about), and give the subject/patient all the space in the analytic setting. In other words, there is only the patient and his past that is supposed to be active in a relation with the analyst. This is the framework that allows transference to clearly take place and become interpretable. The unconscious material will inevitably appear and get interpreted. However, it has to be the patient's material uncontaminated by the analyst's disclosure of his thoughts.

Interpersonal relations with patients open the gate for acting-out preconscious thoughts and lead to scenes of *follie à deux*. The common confused relational situations in the sessions come from two transferences[4] engaged in a futile effort to find a place in the clinical setup. The analytic work of interpretation and reconstruction seizes to happen in those cases, because of the absence of differentiation between analyst and patient. Both analyst and analysand have and produce manifestations of themselves. The psychoanalyst's manifest is expected to be more stable and relates to a steady content. The patient's manifest is likely to change with the progress of analysis; the content will not change radically but will adapt to the new healthier manifest. However, in relational psychotherapy both analyst and analysand act out their own transferences. The present or the manifest becomes a scene of enactment of two unknown and foreign 'latents,' and likely suggests two pathological contents.

---

[3] Discovering transference (1912b) and working with / it is one of the difficult things in the practice of psychoanalysis, and is the most differentiating feature that distinguishes psychoanalysis from any other psychotherapies.

[4] Counter transference is a misnomer and misleading term. The analyst's relation with his patient is, in general, influenced by the quality and degree of his training. He reacts to the patient within his abilities to practice psychoanalysis properly. Therefore, the patient's transference is not supposed to provoke a special 'counter action' in the analyst to call it counter transference, unless the analyst is not trained well or lacks experience.

In proper clinical practice of psychoanalysis, the parameters of the analytic relationship and the conditions under which the analysis will be practiced are very important to impart to the patient from the very beginning, and to be explained so that he will not consider them as the parameters of a real relationship with the analyst. This point is not a matter of preference or convenience; it is an integral part of the theory of the subject. The setup of psychoanalysis in regard to the number of sessions, duration of the session, cancellation, missing sessions, being late or early, vacations, payments, duration of a psychoanalysis, termination, and whatever might happen during a long relationship have to be discussed with the patient in advance. Any possible or foreseen changes should also be discussed and considered. *The analytic conditions should be specified, presented, explained, and emphasized to the patients before starting psychoanalyzing.*

Another aspect of informing the patient from the beginning of the psychoanalytic setup is to emphasize that coming for the sessions few times a week for a long period is still to do work in every one of those sessions. It is natural that the patient – and the analyst – would get into the habit of meeting and the purpose of those meetings would fade away with time. Having and maintaining clear different parameters for the relationship with the analyst is the safeguard against slaking off in doing the job of analysis and of being merely a patient.

Freud's Insight and the Issue of Training

The guidelines and the rules of establishing training traditions were decided at an early phase of the movement. There was a great demand for training and there were only few analysts who could be entrusted with task of training. Many of the candidates were not Europeans and most of the Europeans were out of town where training was happening. The four and five sessions a week for didactic analysis and for a short time was the norm to free the training analysts to take new candidates. However, we know now that the theory of the subject supports the principle of didactic analysis, but has nothing to say about the number of sessions per week or per an analysis. Theoretically, *frequent and stable number of sessions is required but anything else is to be decided by the conditions of the patients (diagnosis), circumstances, and the subject's capabilities. Analysis is determined by the patient, not by the theory or the analyst's preferences.*

When training expanded outside Vienna and became the agreed upon international wright to join the discipline, the tradition of the didactic analysis was preserved but was given a new name and function. It became a personal analysis for therapeutic purposes. Its intensity (four and five sessions per week) that came from the short but intensified period of early training was preserved and justified by the new therapeutic purposes. Furthermore, the additional contributions to the theory from the new generation of analysts extended the training phase. Personal analysis extended to equal the length of training period. Changes happened gradually and quietly and under the watching eye of IPA and *the training analysts*. But the most curious thing is extending the principle of the four\five sessions demanded of the candidates to the analysis of patients. It was almost implicitly said that what is therapeutic for the analyst should also be what is therapeutic for the patient. No one asked questions about the 'logic' of those unwavering traditions. Analysts and patients alike do not question entrenched traditions, especially in psychoanalysis, to avoid being asked to explain their asking.

If we follow the basic premises of analyzing the intrapsychic manifested in the subject's dualities, interpreting transference material to reveal the implicit unconscious in it, and do the work of reconstruction in the process, we should not apply blindly a certain modality of practice regarding the frequency of session and the duration of an analysis. A responsible clinician should do a proper diagnosis to decide if psychoanalysis is the right approach for that particular patient. If the patient is right for psychoanalysis, his circumstance[5] has to be discussed with him to come to an agreement regarding the frequency of sessions per week. It is important to highlight this point, because both analyst and analysand should always look at the analytic work as a project, a mission, or an undertaking that has to be brought to an end, and not just a new relationship required to initiate psychotherapeutic changes. Psychoanalysts are not healers; they have a defined job to do, a defined way to do it, and it will be determined by their training and their abilities.

Therefore, we could and should go to Freud's intuition regarding the practice of psychoanalyzing and question the present way psychoanalysis is practiced.

---

[5] What is meant by circumstances is the patient's own feeling about the gravity, pressure, need for expedited therapy, and then the material circumstances of the patient.

Epilogue

The four fundamental discoveries of psychoanalysis (mentioned above) are not enough to qualify psychoanalysis as a human science, in the literal meaning of science. However, they force us to deal with two important issues related to the future of psychoanalysis. The first is that when psychoanalysis is considered a science, it will be our responsibility to itemize it into topics to study, learn, and train. Itemizing psychoanalysis as topics will show and prove that a program in psychoanalysis requires the input of several branches of the humanities (Freud, 1926 e). Putting all that together would make it clear that the present system of training is too simplistic, insufficient, narrow in scope, and goes against the direction psychoanalysis should be taking in the future. Becoming a science that has applications suggests strongly that training in psychoanalysis has to be a full-time concern; it will comprise selective subjects and different majors and multiple supplemental courses, defined responsibilities that are accountable to the teaching faculty (the training analysts of today) and the trainees. It will become a very involved matter. Most of all, it will make the future analyst develop his identity as a psychoanalyst, not as a mental health provider.

A natural evolution of psychoanalysis requires learning psychoanalysis in academic establishments, in academic institutions, and in ways that are appropriate to the standards of training in the other academic professional fields like education, medicine, and psychology. In the first place, preset psychoanalytic knowledge – even if limited to its clinical aspect – needs more than the part time programs offered in the IPA regular institutes. It is also getting more involved in different types of psychopathologies that are not totally of psychodynamic origin or are *falsely* related to relational issues. The training aspect in psychoanalysis is still following the limited and traditional way of transmitting experience from an experienced practitioner to a younger practitioner, as it was the tradition in the middle ages. Training in any profession is better done in academia because many of the issues of choosing the training faculty, the standers of training, the certification and licensing procedures are better dealt with in institutions that have the experience and tradition of handling those matters, and stop the uncontrollable and mismanaged way pervasive in IPA training institutes.

Modern Psychoanalysis and the Issue of Training

The second issue is the current crisis of psychoanalysis. There is no mention of the nature of that crisis, except in how it is affecting the practice and practitioners of psychoanalysis. Moreover, there is no clear agreement on its cause, or any possible solutions. The reason, in my opinion, is that the background of psychoanalysts is three divergent disciplines and with three different basic trainings. The IPA's acceptance of training those divergent candidates with the same program in the same institutes means that IPA simply considers its training programs and training institutes a place to acquire a *skill* not to learn something, if not anything about the subject matter of the acquired skill to do psychotherapy. It also means that it is sufficient to create psychoanalysts irrespective of their previous academic graduate and postgraduate formation. This implies disregard, even disdain, of psychoanalysis itself. It is not unimportant – actually it is essential and necessary – to rethink what is happening now to the teaching and training of candidates. There should be serious reviews of learning the vast knowledge we gathered and accumulated in the last hundred years to be compacted in few hours a week, few weeks a year, and for *very* few years.

Another puzzling matter regarding the formation of psychoanalysts is the reason the IPA institutes require the candidate to have obtained a post-graduate degree in a mental health profession. There is no connection between psychoanalysis – even as the only a technique in psychotherapy – and a Ph.D. in psychology or social work or an MD. The only justification for stipulating these prerequisites for training is to have a license to work with patients.

But, how to turn a method of psychotherapy into an academic science?

Psychoanalysis and Academia

The fact of the matter is that psychoanalysis is *not* in a crisis; it is the institutions of psychoanalysis that are in the crisis. Its system of 'institute training' no longer graduates good analysts, and is not showing any signs of awareness of that fact[1]. Analysts of the past knew all that was there to know in

---

[1] Within my limited circle of colleagues, the general mood is anxiety about the dropping numbers of patients and trainees who need personal analysis and supervision. There is total denial that the quality of contemporary psychoanalysis is not conducive to training good analysts. This would naturally show in their

the field, but analysts and faculty of nowadays are in a quandary: teach and learn the classical theory or the new theoretical suggestions? They cannot and do not need do both in the same period of time allotted for training in the institute system is. Moreover, keeping training a property of the IPA institutes, and a private effort of psychoanalysts, obviate consistency and allows for many undesirable deviations in the formation of analysts. Keeping psychoanalysis separate from academia, which is now the natural place of systematic learning of any knowledge, disadvantages psychoanalysis by branding it as trade or a skill.

If we accept that the poor learning and training is the cause of the crisis of psychoanalysis, we could envisage how to go about solving the problem. All the attempts to improve the existing system have failed. Thus, the solution has to be getting out of our isolation, joining the scientific march that starts from academia and encompasses all the humanities.

The transition from the IPA to the academic system is the problem because analysts got habituated to being unique, self-contained, and private community. We also have rooted disdain for anything that is not – let alone against – clinical 'psychoanalytic matters.' If there is a problem with the status of the training analyst it is attaching to training an implicit narcissistic mentality of superiority and distinction, which characterizes the psychoanalysts' self-image. This unhealthy and mostly unconscious part of training in psychoanalysis would not have a chance to last in academia beyond the limits of the classrooms.

---

practice and would discourage patients from seeking psychoanalysts for psychotherapy. Naturally too, this will lower the interest of the young professional in going through a long and expensive training that has no better results.

Index

References

Althusser, L, (1996). Psychoanalysis the Human Sciences, S. Randell (Trans.), New Your, Colombia University Press.

Blass, R. (2002). *The Meaning of the Dream in Psychoanalysis*. New York: State University of New York Press.

Cambridge, MA & London: The Belknap Press of Harvard University Press.

Bion W. (1965). *Learning from Experience*, Lanham & Oxford, Rowman &Littlefield Publishers.

Bion, W. (1988). *Attention and Interpretation*, London, Karnak.

Brenner, C. *The Mind in Conflict*, New York, International University Press.

Calaprice, A. (2000). The Expanded Quotable Einstein by Einstein, Princeton, Princeton University Press,

Cassirer, E. (1953). *An Essay on Man*, Doubleday Anchor, New York.

Cesio, F. (1995). Report to the House of Delegates' Committee on "*The Actual Crisis of Psychoanalysis: Challenges and Perspectives.*" International Psychoanalytic Association Publications.

Christian, D. (2018). Origin Story, A History of Everything, New York, Little Brown and company.

Compton, A. (1981a). On the psychoanalytic theory of instinctual drives, *The Psychoanalytic Quarterly*, 50, 190–218.

Compton, A. (1981b). On the psychoanalytic theory of instinctual drives, *The Psychoanalytic Quarterly,* 50, 219–237.

Compton, A. (1981c). On the psychoanalytic theory of instinctual drives, *The Psychoanalytic Quarterly*, 50, 345–262.

Compton, A. (1981d). On the Psychoanalytic Theory of instinctual dives, *The Psychoanalytic Quarterly*, 50, 363–392

Damasio, A. R. (2003). *Looking for Spinoza: Joy, Sorrow and the Feeling Brain (A Harvest Book)*. New York: Harcourt.

De Saussure, F. (1997). *Course in General Linguistics*, Open Court Publishing Company, ninth edition, Peru, Illinois.

Descartes, R. (1999). *Discourse on Method and Related Writings*. (D. Clarke, Trans.). London: Penguin Books. (Original work published 1637).

Edwards, P. Encyclopedia of Philosophy , New York, Macmillan Publishing Co. & Free press.

Elder, C. (1994). *The Grammar of the Unconscious: A Conceptual Foundation of Psychoanalysis*. Pennsylvania: Pennsylvania University Press.

Erickson, E. (1950). Childhood and Society, New York, Norton.

Fayek, A. (2002). Psychic reality and mental representation. *Psychoanalytic Psychology*, 19, 475–500.

Fayek, A. (2010). *The Crisis in Psychoanalysis*, Austin, Texas. Bridgehead Books.

Fayek, A. (2013). *Freud's Other Theory of Psychoanalysis: The Replacement of the Indelible Cathartic Theory.* New York, Jason Aronson.

Fayek, A. (2015). *Future Psychoanalysis, Toward a Psychology of the Human Subject.* New York, Rowman & Littlefield Publishing

Freud, S. (1900 a). *The Interpretation of Dreams. Standard Edition*, Vol. 4–5. London: The Hogarth Press and the Institute of Psycho-Analysis.

Freud, S. (1901 b). *The Psychopathology of Everyday Life, Standard Edition*, Vol. 6, London: The Hogarth Press and the Institute of Psycho-Analysis.

Freud, S. (1905 c). *Jokes and Their Relation to the Unconscious Standard Edition*, Vol. 6, London: The Hogarth Press and the Institute of Psycho-Analysis.

Freud, S. (1905 d). *Three Essays on the Theory of Sexuality. Standard Edition,* Vol. 7. London: The Hogarth Press and the Institute of Psycho-Analysis.

Freud, S. (1910 K). "Wild" Psycho-Analysis, *Standard Edition*, Vol. 11, 221, London: The Hogarth Press and the Institute of Psycho-Analysis.

Freud, S. (1912 b). Dynamics of Transference, Vol.12, 99, *Standard Edition*, Vol. 1, 213. London: The Hogarth Press and the Institute of Psycho-Analysis.

Freud. S. (1912 e). Recommendations to Physicians Practicing Psycho-Analysis, *Standard Edition*, Vol. 12,111, London: The Hogarth Press and the Institute of Psycho-Analysis. Freud, S.

(1912 g). A note on the unconscious. *Standard Edition*, Vol. 12, 121–144. London: The Hogarth Press and the Institute of Psycho-Analysis.

Freud, S. (1913 c). On the Beginning of Treatment (Further Recommendations on the Technique of Psycho-Analysis, I), *Standard Edition*, Vol. 12,123. London: The Hogarth Press and the Institute of Psycho-Analysis.

Freud, S. (1914 c). On narcissism: An introduction. *Standard Edition*, Vol. 14, 67–104. London: The Hogarth Press and the Institute of Psycho-Analysis.

Freud, S. (1914 g). Remembering, Repeating and Working Through (Further Recommendations on the technique of the Technique of Psycho-Analysis, II), Vol. 12, 147. *Standard Edition*, Vol. 1, 213. London: The Hogarth Press and the Institute of Psycho-Analysis.

Freud, S. (1915 a). Instincts and their vicissitude. *Standard Edition*, Vol. 14, 109–140. London: The Hogarth Press and the Institute of Psycho-Analysis.

Freud, S. (1915c). The unconscious. *Standard Edition*, Vol. 14, 159–204. London: The Hogarth Press and the Institute of Psycho-Analysis.

Freud, S. (1915 d). Repression. *Standard Edition*, Vol. 14, 141–158. London: The Hogarth Press and the Institute of Psychoanalysis.

Freud, S. (1915 e). The unconscious. *Standard Edition*, Vol. 14, 159–204. London: The Hogarth Press and the Institute of Psycho-Analysis.

Freud, S. (1916–1917). *Introductory Lectures on Psychoanalysis.* *Standard Edition*, Vol. 15–16. London: The Hogarth Press and the Institute of Psycho-Analysis

Freud, S. (1918 b). From the history of infantile neurosis, *Standard Edition*, Vol. 17, 1–123. London: The Hogarth Press and the Institute of Psycho-Analysis.

Freud, S. (920g). *Beyond the Pleasure Principle*, Freud, S., *Standard Edition*, Vol. 18, 3–65. London: The Hogarth Press and the Institute of Psycho-Analysis.

Freud, S. (1923b). *The Ego and the Id. Standard Edition*, Vol. 19, 1–58. London: The Hogarth Press and the Institute of Psycho-Analysis.

Freud, S. (1925 h). Negation, London: *Standard Edition*, Vol. 19, 235–240.Th e Hogarth Press and the Institute of Psycho-Analysis

Freud, S. (1926 e). The question of lay analysis. *Standard Edition*, Vol. 20, 177–250. London: The Hogarth Press and the Institute of Psycho-Analysis.

Freud, S. (1933a). *New Introductory Lectures on Psychoanalysis* (lectures XXIX–XXXV). *Standard Edition*, Vol. 22. London: The Hogarth Press and the Institute of Psycho-Analysis.

Freud, S. (1937d). Construction in psychoanalysis. *Standard Edition*, Vol. 23, 255–270. London: The Hogarth Press and the Institute of Psycho-Analysis.

Freud, S. (1913 c). On the Beginning of Treatment (Further Recommendations on the Technique of Psycho-Analysis, I), *Standard Edition*, Vol. 12,123. London: The Hogarth Press and the Institute of Psycho-Analysis.

Freud, S. (1914 c). On narcissism: An introduction. *Standard Edition*, Vol. 14, 67–104. London: The Hogarth Press and the Institute of Psycho-Analysis.

Freud, S. (1914 g). Remembering, Repeating and Working Through (Further Recommendations on the technique of the Technique of Psycho-Analysis, II), Vol. 12, 147. *Standard Edition*, Vol. 1, 213. London: The Hogarth Press and the Institute of Psycho-Analysis.

Freud, S. (1915 a). Instincts and their vicissitude. *Standard Edition*, Vol. 14, 109–140. London: The Hogarth Press and the Institute of Psycho-Analysis.

Freud, S. (1915c). The unconscious. *Standard Edition*, Vol. 14, 159–204. London: The Hogarth Press and the Institute of Psycho-Analysis.

Freud, S. (1915 d). Repression. *Standard Edition*, Vol. 14, 141–158. London: The Hogarth Press and the Institute of Psychoanalysis.

Freud, S. (1915 e). The unconscious. *Standard Edition*, Vol. 14, 159–204. London: The Hogarth Press and the Institute of Psycho-Analysis.

Freud, S. (1916–1917). *Introductory Lectures on Psychoanalysis*. *Standard Edition*, Vol. 15–16. London: The Hogarth Press and the Institute of Psycho-Analysis

Freud, S. (1918 b). From the history of infantile neurosis, *Standard Edition*, Vol. 17, 1–123. London: The Hogarth Press and the Institute of Psycho-Analysis.

Freud, S. (920g). *Beyond the Pleasure Principle*, Freud, S., *Standard Edition*, Vol. 18, 3–65. London: The Hogarth Press and the Institute of Psycho-Analysis.

Freud, S. (1923b). *The Ego and the Id. Standard Edition*, Vol. 19, 1–58. London: The Hogarth Press and the Institute of Psycho-Analysis.

Freud, S. (1925 h). Negation, London: *Standard Edition*, Vol. 19, 235–240.Th e Hogarth Press and the Institute of Psycho-Analysis

Freud, S. (1926 e). The question of lay analysis. *Standard Edition*, Vol. 20, 177–250. London: The Hogarth Press and the Institute of Psycho-Analysis.

Freud, S. (1933a). *New Introductory Lectures on Psychoanalysis* (lectures XXIX–XXXV). *Standard Edition*, Vol. 22. London: The Hogarth Press and the Institute of Psycho-Analysis.

Freud, S. (1937d). Construction in psychoanalysis. *Standard Edition*, Vol. 23, 255–270. London: The Hogarth Press and the Institute of Psycho-Analysis.

Freud, S. (1940a). An outline of Psychoanalysis, *Standard Edition*, Vol. 23, 141-279. London: The Hogarth Press and the Institute of Psycho-Analysis.

Freud, S. (1950a [1887–1902]). *Project for a Scientific Psychology*. *Standard Edition*, Vol. 1. London: The Hogarth Press and the Institute of Psycho-Analysis.

Green, A., (1999). The Fabric of Affect in the Psychoanalytic Discourse, A. Sheridan (trans). London, Routledge.

Gesell, A. (1940).*The First Five Years of Life*, A guide to the study of Preschool Child, New York, Mathuen.Grunberger, B. (1979). *Narcissism: psychoanalytic essay*, J. Diamenti & O. Olinar, Trans.). New York, International University Press (Original work 19710.

Harari, Y.N (2016). *Sapiens: A Brief History of Mankind*, McClelland &Stewart, Canada

Heidrich, T. (2005). Oxford Companion to Philosophy, Oxford, Oxford University Press.

Holder, A. (1970). *Instinct and drive*. In H. Garma (Ed.), Basic Psychoanalytic Concepts on the Theory of Instincts (Vol. III).

Issacs, S. (1952). The nature and function of phantasy. In M. Klein (Ed.), *Developments in Psychoanalysis*. London: Hogarth Press.

Jones, E. (1954). *Sigmund Freud: Life and work* (Vol. 1). London: Hogarth Press.

King, P, & Steiner R. (1991). *The Freud-Klein Controversies* 1941–1945, London, Routledge.

Levi-Strauss, C. (1955). The structural study of the myth, *Journal of American Folklore*, 68, 113–144.

Levi-Strauss, C. (1963). *Structural Anthropology,* New York, Basic Books.

Laplanche, J. (1989). *New Foundation for Psychoanalysis*, (D. Macey, Trans) Oxford, Blackwell.

Hegel, P. (1987). Introduction to the Lectures of History of Philosophy, T.M. Knox. A.V. Miller (trans). Oxford, Oxford University Press.

Lacan, J. (1977). Ecrits: Selections (A Sheridan Trans.) New York, Norton and Company

Laplanche, J. (1992). Interpretation between determinism and hermeneutics. A restatement of the problem. *The International Journal of Psychoanalysis*, 73, 429–446.

Laplanche, J., & Pontalis, J-B. (1973). *The language of psychoanalysis*. (D. Nicholson-Smith, Trans.). New York: Norton. (Original work published 1967

Masson, J.M., (1985). *The Complete Letters of Freud to Fliess*, 1887–1904Matte-Blanco, M. I. (1975). *The Unconscious as Infinite Sets: An Essay in Bi-Logic*. London, Duckworth.

Matte-Blanco, I. (1988). *Thinking, feeling, and being (A Tavistock Professional Book)*. London and New York: Routledge

Moreno, J. (1987). Essential Moreno Writings in psychodrama, Group Methods, and Spontaneity, New York, Springer publishing Company Nasio,

J-D. (1984). The unconscious, the transference, and the psychoanalyst's interpretation: A Lacanian view. *The Psychoanalytic Inquiry*, 4, 401–411.

Natterson, J.M., Friedman, R.J. (1995). *A Primer of Clinical Intersubjectivity*, New York, Rowman & Littlefield Publishers.

Oxford Dictionary of Philosophy (2005). Oxford, Oxford University Press.

Piaget, J. (1955), *Language and Thought Of the Child*, New York, Meridian Books.

Politzer, G. (1994–1928). *Critique of the Foundation of Psychology*. (A. Appry, Trans.). Pittsburgh: Duguene University Press. (Original work published 1928).

Rawls, J. (2000). Lectures on the History of Moral Philosophy, Barbara Herman (ed), London, Massachusetts, Harvard University Press.

Renick, O. (1993). Analytic interaction: conceptualizing technique in light of the analyst's irreducible subjectivity, *Psychoanalytic Quarterly*, 62, 553-571,

Renick, O. (1995). The ideal of the anonymous analyst and the problem of self-disclosure, *Psychoanalytic Quarterly*, 64,466-495.

Renick, O. (1996). The perils of neutrality. *Psychoanalytic Quarterly*, 65, 495–517.

Renick, O. (1998). Getting real in analysis, *Psychoanalytic Quarterly*, LXVII, 566–593.

Renick. O. (2007), Intersubjectivity, therapeutic action, and analytic technique, Psychoanalytic Quarterly 76-S, 1547–1562.

Ricoeur, P. (1970). *Freud and Philosophy: An essay on interpretation.* (D. Savage, Trans.). New Haven: Yale University Press

Roudinesco, E. (2016). *Freud: In His Time and Ours*, (C. Porter, Trans). Cambridge Massachusetts, Harvard University Press.

Russell, B. (1967). *History of Western Philosophy*, New York, Simon & Schuster.

Simons, R. (1981). Panel, Contemporary problems of psychoanalysis, *Journal of the American Psychoanalytic Associations*, 22, 643657.

Stolorow, R, Orang, D.M., Atwood, G.E., (2001). Psychoanalysis Without Descartes, *The International Journal of Psychoanalysis,* 82:1263–1266.

Storolow, R., Atwood, G.E., Brandchaft, B. (2012) ed. Intersubjective Perspectives, Lanham, Oxford, Jason Aronson Books.

Tripp, E. (1970). *The Meridian Handbook of Classical Mythology.* New York, New American Library.

Waelder, R. (1941–1942). *"On psychoanalytic technique: Five lectures."* In Guttman, S., & Guttman, I., with the assistance of I. K. Guttman (1987). *Psychoanalytic Quarterly*, XLVI, 1–68.

Wallerstein, R. (1998). Psychoanalysis, The Common Grounds, The International Journal Of psychoanalysis, 71, 3-20.

Wallerstein, R. (2005). Will Psychoanalytic Plurality be an Enduring State of our Discipline? *The international Journal of Psychoanalysis*, 86,623-

Wallheim, R. (1993). *The Mind in its Depth*. Cambridge, MA: Harvard University Press.

Wicks, R. (2014). *Kant: A Complete Introduction*. USA, McGrow Hill companies.

Wittgenstein, L. (1982/1948–49). *The Last Writings on the Philosophy of Psychology* (Vol. 1), (G. H. von Wright & H. Nyman, Eds.; C. G. Lockhart & M. A. E. Aue, Trans.). Chicago: University of Chicago Press. (Original work published 1982).

Zagermann. (2017). The Future of Psychoanalysis: The debate About the Training Analyst System, Ed. Zagermann, London, Karnak.

www.ingramcontent.com/pod-product-compliance
Lightning Source LLC
Chambersburg PA
CBHW050228270326
41914CB00003BA/621